AGNIPARIKSHA

Hamid Kureshi (1927–2016), a Gujarat High Court advocate and Gandhian, was the chairman of the Sabarmati Ashram Preservation and Memorial Trust, Ahmedabad. He was the grandson of Abdul Kadir Bawazeer, a close friend and lifelong associate of M. K. Gandhi. He published *Agnipariksha* in 2003.

Rita Kothari is Professor of English, Ashoka University, Sonepat, Haryana. A cultural historian, writer and translator, her published works include *The Burden of Refuge* (2009), *Memories and Movements* (2013), and *A Multilingual Nation* (2017).

Narayan Desai (1924–2015) the son of Mahadev Desai, Gandhi's personal secretary and biographer, was a Gandhian, peace activist, educator and writer. *Gandhi Through a Child's Eyes* (1992), *Story of a Gandhian Educator* (1997), and *My Life Is My Message* (2009) are some of his works.

Gandhi Studies

The life and thought of Mahatma Gandhi are intertwined and inseparable. His politics was imbued with his spiritual experiments and his spirituality was tempered by his vision of a non-violent society, and his constructive work was integral to his politics. The unique practices of Gandhi, his control of palate, his fasts, his spinning, his silence and his prayers were sustained and nurtured by the ashrams that he founded. The ashram community through its own practices affirmed, modified and validated Gandhi's ideals and practices.

Gandhi Studies aspires to examine and elucidate the relationship between life and thought, between experiment and practice, and between Gandhi and the institutions he founded and the experiments he inspired. Biographical studies of Gandhi and his associates, histories of institutions and ideas, along with translations of scholarly and memoir literature from various Indian languages will form part of this endeavour. This series is committed to no one fixed way of understanding Gandhi; it hopes like Gandhi himself to be deeply dialogic.

In the series

Beloved Bapu: The Gandhi-Mirabehn Correspondence (Edited and introduced by Tridip Suhrud and Thomas Weber)

Soulmates: The Story of Mahatma Gandhi and Hermann Kallenbach, Shimon Lev

Speaking of Gandhi's Death (Edited by Peter Ronald deSouza and Tridip Suhrud)

M. K. Gandhi's Hind Swaraj: A Critical Edition (Annotated, translated and edited by Suresh Sharma and Tridip Suhrud)

My Life is My Message, Narayan Desai (Translated by Tridip Suhrud)

Notes from Gandhigram: Challenges to Gandhian Praxis, Samir Banerjee

Rethinking Gandhi and Nonviolent Relationality: Global Perspectives (Edited by Debjani Ganguly and John Docker)

The Shanti Sena: Philosophy, History and Action, Thomas Weber

Gandhi's Khadi: A History of Contention and Conciliation, Rahul Ramagundam

Harilal Gandhi: A Life, Chandulal Bhagubhai Dalal (Translated by Tridip Suhrud)

In the Tracks of the Mahatma: The Making of a Documentarym A. K. Chettiar (Edited by A. R. Venkatachalapathy and translated by S. Thillainayagam)

AGNIPARIKSHA
An Ordeal Remembered

Hamid Kureshi

Translated from the original Gujarati by
RITA KOTHARI

With a Foreword by
NARAYAN DESAI

Orient BlackSwan

AGNIPARIKSHA: AN ORDEAL REMEMBERED

ORIENT BLACKSWAN PRIVATE LIMITED

Registered Office
3-6-752 Himayatnagar, Hyderabad 500 029, Telangana, India
e-mail: centraloffice@orientblackswan.com

Other Offices
Bangalore, Bhopal, Chennai, Guwahati,
Hyderabad, Jaipur, Kolkata, Lucknow, Mumbai,
New Delhi, Noida, Patna, Vijayawada

Originally published in Gujarati as
Agnipariksha (Ahmedabad: Gurjar Granthratna Karyalaya, 2003).

026651

ISBN 978-93-5287-196-4

Typeset in
Minion Pro 11.5/13.5
by Manmohan Kumar, Delhi

Printed in India at
Yash Printographics, Noida

Published by
Orient Blackswan Private Limited
3-6-752, Himayatnagar Hyderabad 500 029
e-mail: info@orientblackswan.com

CONTENTS

LIST OF IMAGES

FOREWORD

Good literature is one that gives voice to human suffering, reflects the miseries of a society, and its expression must be such that after awakening sensitivity to pain, it also finds a way to heal it. When pain is unaccompanied by consciousness, it brings numbness and when pain finds no means of healing, it brings death. Good literature removes numbness and rescues humans from death by taking them towards immortality. Hamid Kureshi's personal account, his *aap-veeti*, is not only an account of pain, or *veetak-katha*, but also good literature.

Ahmedabad had witnessed communal riots prior to independence, but since independence it has become a particularly frequent victim of communalism. There are many sides to communal strife—economic, sectarian, political etc. However all these aspects collectively affect the human aspect. With every riot, humanity descends to a lower level. At the cost of most, a few manage to get financial advantage out of riots. At the price of democracy, some sections get emboldened; at the cost of dharma, sectarian factions raise their heads. But with every riot, it is humanity that loses.

However, the hallmark of humankind is to rise after every fall and such is human nature that it can, even while facing the jaws of death, hand out *sanjeevni*, the cure to mortality. Hamidbhai has presented his experiences with great restraint and yet managed to highlight acts of sensitivity and compassion in the midst of rage, hatred and suffering. He has described shocking incidents in a sparse and forgiving manner, avoiding an exuberance of metaphors. He has related instances of love and affection with utmost gratitude and warmth. The salient characteristics of Hamid Kureshi's style are his restraint and balance which make his narrative more effective. This story of humanity is a welcome addition to humanitarian literature.

Narayan Desai

AUTHOR'S PREFACE

Imam Saheb (Abdul Kadir Bawazeer) met Mahatma Gandhi in South Africa in the year 1903. Drawn by Gandhiji's personality and principles, he abandoned home and livelihood and joined the Gandhian movement along with his family. He became a resident of the Phoenix Ashram. Gandhiji honoured him with the title '*Sahodar*' [literally, born of the same womb]. He was like a brother to Gandhiji.

In the year 1915 Gandhiji left South Africa and returned to India. Imam Saheb did the same. He returned home with his wife Haji Saheba and their daughters Fateema and Ameena (my mother). Imam Saheb spent the rest of his life as Gandhiji's close companion and trusted friend. Until his death in 1931, he lived at the Ashram. The house built for him in the precincts of the Ashram is called Imam Manzil.

In the year 1924, Ameenaben married Ghulam Rasool Kureshi, a young man inspired by Gandhiji. He was a Muslim nationalist from Dhandhuka, Gujarat, and had joined the Gandhian struggle for independence. The marriage took place in the Gandhi Ashram. Since then, Imam Manzil became the permanent residence of the Kureshi family.

We are the children of Ghulam Rasool Kureshi and Ameenaben: Sultanaben, Hamid and Waheed. All three of us were born and raised in Imam Manzil.

Shri Harjivandas Kotak and Shrimati Shardaben Kotak were inmates at the Gandhi Ashram. They had four daughters: Pratima, Gira, Sumitra and Hansa. I, Hamid Kureshi, was married to Pratima. I became part of the Kotak family. We had two daughters, Shamim and Yasmin, and three sons, Aabid, Munir and Akil.

My younger brother Waheedbhai married Laila, the daughter of Ismailbhai Nagori, a well-known Gandhian from Saurashtra. They have four daughters—Naseem, Meena, Ruab, Shireen—and a son, Naasir.

During the Gandhi centennial of 1969, this was our family, our community, our *kutumbh-kabilo*. We lived in our home 'Akil Villa' in Swastik Society. Waheedbhai's family lived in the University area.

In September of 1969, communal riots broke out in the city. Our extended family included the following: my closest friend Madhavsinhbhai Solanki; mentor and father-like Jhinabhai Desai; family friend and well-wisher Shri Surabhai Bharwad; Mohanbhai Patel who was like a member of the family; leading Gandhian activist and source of inspiration Shri Dhirubhai Desai. It also extended to Mrs. Ushaben Gandhi, Ashokbhai Naik, inhabitants of Swastik Society, Shri Mansingh Dodiya and all the inmates of Gandhi Ashram.

The flames leaping out of the riots scorched us as well. We also had the opportunity to come face-to-face with love and human sanctity. What I saw, learnt and experienced got written down during those days, and that is what I present here.

Hamid Kureshi

PEOPLE IN THE BOOK

Bhanubhai Thakker: The owner of the house occupied by Hamid Kureshi's brother Waheedbhai in the University area in Ahmedabad.

Chhaganbhai Joshi: A resident of Gandhi Ashram, chief worker of the Gausewa Sangh and Harijan welfare activities, and participant in the Dandi March led by Gandhi.

Dahyabhai Nayak: A committed tribal activist and administrator of Gandhi Ashram.

Dattubhai Maha: An inmate of Gandhi Ashram and a well-known sculptor and painter.

Dhirubhai Desai: A social worker hailing from Agasi, Chikhli taluka, Surat, an educator and follower of the Gandhian idea of constructive activism.

Dilkhushbhai Diwanji: A leading activist in the campaign for khadi and the Indian freedom movement in Gujarat.

Dr. Anil Patel: An inmate of Gandhi Ashram and a journalist.

Dr. O. P. Gupta: Superintendent, Civil Hospital, Ahmedabad.

Dr. Pushpendra Bhatt: Municipal Corporator and member of the Swastik Society residential colony, Ahmedabad, and a doctor by profession.

Dr. Trivedi: A resident of Gandhi Ashram and veterinary expert associated with the Ashram Gaushala.

Ishwarbhai Amin: A volunteer at Gandhi Ashram and in-charge of the Ashram Gaushala.

Jhinabhai Desai: An acclaimed Gujarati poet of the Gandhian era known by his pen-name 'Sneharashmi,' a well-known educator and the principal of Sheth Chimanlal Nagindas Vidyavihar school in Ahmedabad.

Kanubhai Vaghela: A volunteer at Gandhi Ashram.

Khimjibhai Patel: A volunteer with the Kalamkhush office at Gandhi Ashram.

Kishanbhai Trivedi: A volunteer at Gandhi Ashram.

Madalsaben: Daughter of the industrialist and staunch Gandhian Jamnalal Bajaj, and wife of Shrimannarayan, then Gujarat Governor.

Madhavsinh Solanki: A leading politician and statesman of Gujarat and then Deputy Chief Minister.

Mansingh Dodiya: Technical expert associated with the production of handmade paper through the Kalamkhush office of Gandhi Ashram, an engineer by profession and longstanding member of the Ashram community.

Mohanbhai Ganeshbhai Patel: Personal assistant to Hamid Kureshi's father Ghulam Rasool Kureshi, and in-charge of khadi activities and Kalamkhush.

Muljibhai Gadhvi: A senior leader of the Gadhvi community, held in great regard by the Kureshi family.

Navalbhai Shah: Former education minister, Gujarat, and follower of the Gandhian ideal of constructive activism.

Ramjibhai Badiya: Eldest member of the first Harijan family at Gandhi Ashram.

Shantibhai Rawal: A social worker and resident of Shantinagar Society.

Surabhai Bharwad: A social worker and leading member of the Bharwad community who contributed to the social awakening of his community.

Vijayaben Desai: Wife of Jhinabhai Desai (Sneharashmi) and a well-known social worker.

Yashwantbhai Shukla: A reputed writer, thinker and educationist.

Friday, 19 September 1969.

2.00 PM. I am at the City Civil Court in Ahmedabad. I wish to conclude my cases here and reach Navrangpura High Court by 2.45 pm. I am in haste.

'There's trouble in the city. Shops are closing down,' I hear someone say. But I am much too busy with my cases to pay attention.

2.30 PM. I sit in my car to go to the High Court. I turn on the ignition. The words that fell on my ears nag me, 'There's trouble in the city... A *tofaan* is brewing.' I did look at the newspaper this morning. I remember reading the headline, 'Jagannath Temple attacked by a mob.' I find my anger rising. What kind of lowly and thoughtless behaviour is this? How can this be acceptable? This was an attack on a sacred place of the Hindus. Shock, anger and sadness engulf me.

Incidents of communal harmony and fellow-feeling in my homeland flash before my eyes. I think of Dr. Zakir Husain, the President of India; Shri Hidayatullah, Chief Justice Supreme Court; Shri Mehndi Nawaz Jung, Governor, Gujarat; and Shri Nomanbhai Miyabhoy, Chief Justice Gujarat High Court. How could one forget the pluralistic, large-hearted nature of this land?

This city, in fact, all of Gujarat was like a beautiful picture that had begun to spoil. If cultured and humane behaviour was to be responded to with sheer barbarism, what was to be expected? The very answer to this question sent shivers through my body.

My car is speeding on the Nehru Bridge. I am moving away from the riot-filled atmosphere of the city towards the safe haven of Navrangpura.

No sign of disquiet here. It's business as usual. The news about shops being closed due to a tense atmosphere appears unfounded. I see students coming out of Nutan Fellowship High School, school bags slung over their shoulders. They seem to be heading home. Perhaps the school administrators were being overcautious and sending them home.

I arrive at the High Court. Everything appears to be normal. After finishing all the tasks at hand I set out for Akil Villa, my home in Swastik Society. In Shishuvihar, the school next door, announcements are being made. The school is about to close.

I reach home. It is almost 5.30 pm. Our youngest son Akil (we call him Bako) enters the compound of our bungalow. Someone is with him. Probably a friend.

Bako, who is nine, comes up to me and gravely says, 'Papa, there are riots in the city. I have brought my friend home. Can we please drop him off to his house? Although the school had ordered a bus for students living in the city, I feel we should drop him home…'

I ask the friend, 'What is your name?'

'Kashyap.'

I smile a rueful smile and say, 'Kashyap, you do know where you have come, right? Do you know who Akil is?'

'He is Muslim,' Kashyap replied, and hastened to add, 'But he is my friend.' His face shone with pride.

6.00 PM. I leave in my car along with Akil and his friend. We drop Kashyap at his home near Bahai Centre in Shahpur. On our way back, we find the streets calm.

8.00 PM. I leave house again. Ahmedabad has its first cricket test match at the Sardar Patel Stadium. I want to know how many tickets Waheedbhai would need so I could arrange for them accordingly. Moreover, it felt like a good idea to go out for a bit. Sports Club, Kamnath Mahadev, St. Xavier's High School, Rajput

Hostel and Pharmacy Hostel—I drive past all of them and arrive at my brother Waheed's place in the University area. Waheedbhai is at his farm in the village of Taravada near Amreli, Saurashtra. At his house here in the city are his wife Laila and their daughters Naseem and Meena. I see a friend of Laila's sitting next to her.

We chat a while. I make haste to return home. Laila insists on serving tea. I tell her, 'It's been a very hectic month. I had to go to Delhi twice. What with both High Court and Supreme Court cases on, I have barely had three hours' sleep at night. Today I have managed to put behind many cases. Madhavsinhbhai had come at six in the morning. We worked on a draft for an hour or so. Several appeals have been typewritten and they need to be perused before I present them in court. For once I am hoping to get a full night's sleep tonight. I dropped by simply to check if you needed tickets for the test match, and how many.'

'Two should be enough.'

I hear some commotion outside. Laila says, 'Bhai, these hostel students have been making strange noises for the past few hours. They are also banging *thalis*. I have a feeling they are at least four hundred in number. Hamidbhai, do you think there's a riot going on?'

'*Arre*, not at all. We went around the city just now. We saw nothing unusual,' I respond, and get ready to leave.

'Would you mind dropping my friend off to her house? It's on your way.'

Laila's friend got into my car and sat next to me.

I drive to Navrangpura via the University library. I see a crowd at some distance. They were probably students, and three or four hundred in number. Some stood watching; others moved about restlessly. They were in pyjamas and vests and some of them had shirts thrown over their pyjamas. Many looked exhausted and sat at the edge of the road while others were ready and armed with rods used for mosquito nets, sticks, pipes, iron rods and stones. They seemed to have grabbed whatever they could lay their hands on and come out on the streets. In anger? To avenge? What?

There are a couple of two-wheelers in front of my car. Are the rioters blocking their way? Surely they are. I slow down and eventually bring the car to a halt. The boys have encircled the entire road now. Some confabulation takes place between the two-wheeler riders and the boys. They stand inspecting something in the diminishing light of dusk. What is going on?

The two-wheelers disperse. Meanwhile ten–fifteen people rush towards the car, raining down rods and lathis. They shout obscenities and I hear odious words such as, 'Find out if he is Hindu or Muslim!' I tremble in fear. 'Arre Bhagwan!' These words escape the lips of Laila's friend who is trying hard not to appear terrified. Someone throws a torchlight on us. Faces peer into the car. I hear a loud crash on the bonnet. My teeth are chattering. I am dressed in white khadi shirt and trousers; it does not look as if I am familiar to any of them. Pairs of eyes dart towards the woman sitting next to me, and come to rest upon the vermillion *chandlo* on her forehead. The boys fidget and slowly they begin to move away. I can see that the sign of her marital status has rescued my life and esteem. This tiny symbol of Hinduism has expanded itself to become my shield. In the midst of horrifying risk, such an amazing safety valve! Divine intervention this must be surely.

At home Pratima too applies the same chandlo on her forehead every morning after her bath. Thoughts of Pratima push their way into my consciousness.

Relieved, safe, I drive on, but not before two large stones come hurtling at us from behind. They crash against the car, and I suspect that one has hit me. I feel a blow on my head and hear my heart pounding. My blood boils. Not just strife, but communal violence? In my own city, in my own locality, my car is stopped and I am wounded?

I am aghast. I swallow my rage and disbelief somehow and drive on. I feel giddy. The trees on both sides of the road seem to move in circles. The lamp posts swirl round and round. Only we remain stationary, or so it appears. The road ahead has begun to recede.

I am still struggling to understand what has happened.

I turn left and drop the lady accompanying me to her house. I was safe because Laila's friend was with me. I turn towards home, grateful to my saviour. It is because of her that I will be reaching home safe today. Indebtedness from some previous birth? But I sense premonitions of an ominous day ahead. I reach home. I get out of my car and seek refuge in my little garden like a wounded bird.

Madhavsinhbhai has arrived. I walk up to where they all stood—Bako, Munno, Aabid and my little daughter Kali.

'Terrible situation in the University area—any bearded man needs to avoid that place.'

Madhavsinhbhai stands lost in thought. 'I don't understand how this is even possible. How can it happen in such a safe locality?'

I am in no mood to argue. He is still wondering while I have just witnessed it, rather, experienced it. I remain silent for fear that my heaving, panting car may speak up any moment and spill the details.

Madhavsinhbhai continues, 'I too saw such rioting. That is why I came here. I passed by the Municipal Market. They had broken into Italian Bakery and Notabene Cleaners and set them alight. I saw boys grabbing biscuits and cakes from the bakery and distributing them, gobbling them up. They are making bonfires with clothes from Notabene. There is daylight robbery going on. I saw all this while walking towards this house. Both shops have flames leaping out of them and spectators have gathered in large numbers to watch. We can both go if you wish to see.'

My mind is in a whirl. Abdul Samad's Italian Bakery and Notabene drycleaners next to it both have been torched! I hear myself telling Madhavsinhbhai, 'We would not like you to go walking. Let's drop you on our way and also have a look around.'

We leave by my car. Near Swastik Crossroad and on the way to Panchvati we see mobs of people screeching and hooting. There are cars, scooters and people on foot. A police van is parked next to Italian Bakery. I see eight to ten cops carrying lathis. Smoke and flames are rising from Notabene Cleaners. Next to it is a large crowd and miscreants in groups of eight to ten. I see them enter the shops, ransack them and leave after adding more fuel to the fire. In the hostel across, people are cheering them on and hooting. The cops are standing by watching the mob, unperturbed. Are these guardians of law or mere dummies, I wonder. They look like khaki puppets to me.

I drive very slowly towards Madhavsinhbhai's house in Sardar Patel Nagar. We drop him off and turn back homewards. By now the crowd next to Italian Bakery has swollen. It is no longer possible to navigate my way to Swastik Crossroad. I try to move back and forth in vain. At this point one of the khaki puppets comes to life and says, 'Saheb, follow us. We will go ahead and make way for you.' My misconception is broken—these are real guardians of law, not khaki puppets.

We follow the police van; other cars follow us. At Swastik Crossroad it is once again difficult to get ahead. The road is filled with angry mobs and the air is thick with cacophonous sounds, like an ocean in fury foaming at its mouth.

10.30 PM. We somehow reach home. Everyone gets off the car in silence. The phone in our living room rings. I pick up the receiver.

'Hamid!' A familiar and mellifluous voice that usually elongates my name endearingly. It was Jhinabhai Desai, the voice of 'Sneharashmi.' But the terseness jars my ears.

'Hamid, you must not stir out of the house. Things don't look good. We, Yashwantbhai Shukla and I, were passing by the University, and we were stopped. They inspected us, recognised us and let us go, but they also threw a stone at the car. *Beta*, times are very bad. Please don't go out anywhere.' His voice was filled with concern.

'*Jee*,' I say, and gently put the receiver back on the cradle.

I am overwhelmed by memories of Jhinabhai's affection. It was 1941, the year of personal satyagraha. My father, Ghulam Rasool Kureshi, was on the verge of political imprisonment. I was then a student of Vidyavihar. Jhinabhai was the principal of the same school.

Once on a Saturday evening, Jhinabhai visited us in Imam Manzil at Gandhi Ashram. He spent the night at our place and left in the morning.

That afternoon my father said to me, 'Jhinabhai had come home especially to tell me that, "If you end up going to jail, there is no need to worry about Hamid. He is my responsibility."'

Jhinabhai's affection for me is limitless. What was his farsighted vision showing him today? By calling me at 10.30 in the night, of which danger was he cautioning me?

11.00 PM. We head to our beds upstairs. Outside, screeching, hooting and yelling can still be heard. I try to sleep, but to no avail. Suddenly, I sit up startled. There is some commotion on the ground floor. I tiptoe towards the window and strain my ears. Pratima has also woken up. She holds me firm by my shoulders. I am unable to move. I sit down. 'You are not going anywhere, promise me,' she says, and she makes me promise in the name of little Akil. 'It's all right,' I say, caressing my sleeping daughter's head as I speak. 'I just thought I heard some sound.'

Far, far away … no, in fact, quite nearby are the rays of a scorching sun. How do I protect her from their glare? I find myself gripped by anxiety and helplessness.

Pratima draws Akil closer. With the core of Hindu faith in her heart, she prays fervently for the safety of her Muslim family. On one hand the ugly face of the riots, the misfortune of witnessing cruelty; on the other the sanctity of this moment. Was I fortunate or unfortunate?

The story of our marriage:

Pratima is Hindu, I a Muslim. Someone had suggested conversion at the time of our wedding. I had protested. We were married under the Special Marriage Act (1872). Pratima was a Hindu, and she remained one. I would take her to the temple.

We raised our children with conviction. Those poor innocents have no idea whether they are Hindu or Muslim.

Years ago, when our eldest daughter Shamim was two, while playing at a neighbour's house, one of the guests there had asked her, 'Beta, who are you? Hindu or Muslim?'

This innocent girl had raised her eyebrows in bewilderment and replied in Hindi, '*Main to Shamim hoon, Shamim*' [I am Shamim. Just Shamim].

Pratima and I are both praying our respective prayers for the safety of our children.

The commotion below has died down. Did it actually happen or was I imagining it all?

Ding…dong…ding… The clock struck 2 am.

The noises outside have subsided. But what of the noises inside? When will those subside? After two hours? Two days? Two years? Or never?

I am haunted by the thought of riots. Scenes from 1941 and 1946 in Ahmedabad flash before my eyes. The coming together of the *Rathyatra* and Friday—scuffles, stabbing, bloodshed, the massacre of innocents. Images marked indelibly on a child's mind toss and turn. After finishing grade three in Gujarat Vidyapeeth I was admitted to C. N. Vidyavihar. Around that time, riots had broken out. Bloodthirsty demons had played havoc with the city of Ahmedabad. The atmosphere was vicious enough to turn even the best into monsters.

During those days, I found two bright students in my class avoiding eye-contact with me. But in the months that followed, affection had returned to those eyes. We became friends. We regarded each other with mutual respect. This friendship has remained intact. All of us cleared our matriculation together. Later, one of the two friends had said to me, 'During the riots we were tempted ... to harm you. Then we got to know you. We felt penitent about our thoughts. You were the only Muslim in a school of seven hundred students. We feared that there might be others like us with the same thoughts crossing their minds. Lest some Hindu boy have nasty ideas like we did and do you any harm, we constantly guarded you and kept vigil over you to protect you.' Those two bright boys who had nursed thoughts of violence during the riots are now eminent doctors of the city, giving new lives to others.

Ding...dong...three...four...

I count up to six. I am reminded of my words to Laila yesterday, 'I am hoping to get a full night's sleep for once.' It is laughable. Neither rest nor sleep. I actually laugh out loud. Surprising. I have heard of tears of joy, but laughter amidst pain and sadness?

It is morning. Almost half past six. Madhavsinhbhai arrives. I talk to him about the ominous things I foresee. He advises me to push away such thoughts, but he too looks worried. He suggests that I bring Laila, Naseem and Meena from the University area over to this house.

Madhavsinhbhai and I reach Waheedbhai's house to fetch Laila and the girls. I tell Laila, 'All of you come home with me.'

'But why though?' asks Laila.

'The situation has worsened. That commotion we heard was the sound of riots. Waheedbhai is also not here. All of you come home with me. Let's lock up this house.'

'We also heard those sounds—the entire night. But Hamidbhai, if we allow such things to frighten us and to make us leave our homes, how will we survive? Fear is not a good idea, right?'

'I am glad you have such courage. But Waheedbhai is not here. As an elder brother it is my duty to take you away. Time demands prudence, not courage.'

Finally Laila agrees to come. Our niece Saida drops by. It appears she must have come by on her way from Gandhi Ashram to her office. How come so early on a Saturday morning, we ask her.

'My school in Memnagar is closed. I saw trouble and flames on the streets. I don't think it's possible for me to go back by bus now,' Saida tells us.

Instead of going home to Swastik Society, we head towards Gandhi Ashram to drop Saida off. At the toll crossroad, next to Navdeep House, we see the Bata Shoe shop broken into, set aflame and robbed. Further ahead, garments from Notabene Cleaners at Usmanpura are being laid out at a chowk for a bonfire. There is no one to stop anyone. Spectators are plenty. We move on. Still further, mattress shops of the Pinjara community are being burnt to ashes. Near Vadaj, right in the middle of the street we see charred, burnt out tyres that must have been used the previous night, the sparks still flying out of them. As I negotiate my car through this searing debris, my nostrils are assaulted by the acrid stench of burning rubber. I feel suffocated. The tyres have almost entirely covered the tarred road. We watch balls of soot rise to the sky.

The shop from where the tyres were looted appears helpless and poor. It has no windows, doors or even a roof. The tall neem tree right next to the shop appears to be struggling free of the night's flames but still caught in its tentacles, its branches burning from top to bottom. We watch wide-eyed these old neighbours, the tyre shop and this neem tree, standing together in a state of ruin.

10.00 AM. We reach Imam Manzil at Gandhi Ashram. Shamim, Mansinghbhai, Chhaganbhai Joshi—all of them anxiously ask after our well-being. Kureshibhai (my father) and Chhaganbhai suggest that we join the peace meeting organised by the Ahmedabad Mayor. Shamim and Mansinghbhai also come along.

On the Ashram Road our car passes through Chandrabhaga, Vadaj and Shantinagar. On the right hand side of Usmanpura is the Sham-e-Burhani Dargah, dating from the times of the Gujarat Sultanate. It is filled with crowds. The usually quiet dilapidated dargah of red stone looks different today. I hear commotion and screams from inside and the sounds of things breaking. Such violence in broad daylight!

We see hordes going towards Kamar Hostel nearby. The whole atmosphere is filled with wrath. I see two policemen on their bicycles coming from the opposite direction across the railway line. Hearing the sounds of stones being pelted at the minaret of the mosque and the screams and shouts of people running, the policemen swiftly turn back. Were they sick of the cacophony and the riots? Instead of moving towards the direction of the trouble, they were moving in the opposite direction. We watch as the two policemen go away in search of a peaceful place where the cries of violated humanity would not reach them.

'Where there is police, there is peace.' I think of the irony of these words and feel it is more in the spirit of: 'Where there is peace, there is police.' Surely they would not be able to say that there was peace where they were. I wondered if the inanimate cops I saw earlier were better than these fugitive ones.

At the Gujarat Vepari Mahamandal we drop Chhaganbhai and Kureshibhai for the citizens' meet, and we head home.

After lunch I go to the High Court. Mansinghbhai is with me. My second appeal is put up on the admission board today. I reach the office of Justice Shri Diwan. Very few lawyers are present. There are hardly any lawyers from the old city. Some have appeared in court without their black gowns. It looks like there is no insistence on formal appearance in the court today. It doesn't look like my appeal stands a chance of discussion today. My turn is still far away. And today is Saturday. Court proceedings will finish by two in the afternoon. It's better to go home.

At the turn out of the High Court, I meet Natubhai coming from the opposite direction. He warns me in a loud voice, 'Don't go towards the city. Master's petrol pump near Shahpur Darwaja has just been torched.'

I turn my gaze towards Shahpur and see black balls of soot rising from that direction. Across the river, a black cloud of smoke hovers over the city. Does it hover on this side of the city as well? Which way is the wind blowing, I don't understand. The columns of smoke seem to permeate the entire sky.

What is happening? I want to know. I want to witness it with my own eyes along with all the adults and children of the family. With this in mind, I go home.

All of us sit in the car and leave. I am at the steering wheel; next to me is Madhavsinhbhai and next to him Mansinghbhai. Pratima and the children are behind. We cross Gandhi Bridge and come to Shahpur.

At the end of the bridge in Shahpur, Master's petrol pump is up in flames. What if the petrol tanker catches fire and explodes? We make haste to leave the spot. At a short distance from the petrol pump is a police station. We see four or five policemen there.

On the way to Delhi Darwaja, a 'khaki puppet' gestures to us not to go any further. I turn the car towards the riverside. From there I pass by Cama Hotel, Khanpur Darwaja, Ritz Hotel and arrive at the Electricity House. We are not allowed to turn left in the direction of Relief Road. The car goes through Congress House and crosses Ellisbridge. Looking back on the left we see clouds of smoke rising higher and higher. Behrampura seems to be afire.

At the Town Hall I turn left. Hordes of people. I see a crowd near Vadilal Hospital. Another laundry across has been attacked. On the streets lie a medley of clothes, papers, chairs etc. My eyes fall on the policemen in the crowd, on the streets and at the police station. Someone lights up the pile of clothes with a match. There is an explosion. Some policemen run in that direction, their movements unmarked by concern or urgency. The riotous mob knows that the police are 'harmless' just as the policemen know they can rely on the mob's 'generosity.' Both seem to have a mutually respectful relationship. It is not possible to go further on Vadilal Road. The crowds are active, the police inactive. The rioters are rampant; the police watch them in silence. There is no safety for ordinary citizens. The guardians of law have sought refuge in the mob's will. I turn right towards Madalpur.

We climb the incline of Pritamnagar and arrive at Sardar Bridge. We slowly go across the river, pass by the Jagannath Temple and move on ahead. It is not possible to go to the temple. Further ahead near the S. T. bus stand are two chawls where Marwaris live. Under the chawls we see frenzied throngs of people. They look purposeful. They are armed with lathis, pipes and rods. They seem to be calling out to someone in the chawl, their eyes bright with fury, their faces taut with demonic purpose.

Shamim, Aabid, Kali, Munno, Bako, Pratima—all are sitting in the rear. My eyes shift from the chawl towards them. Pratima looks away. Mansinghbhai looks tense. My foot instinctively presses down on the accelerator and the car picks up sudden speed. People in the car avert their eyes from what they are made to witness. What is destined to happen will happen. But perhaps we could be spared these nightmarish and hair-raising scenes. We are people in haste.

I turn to the right towards Gita Mandir. I see flames leaping out of shops to my left. Goods from the shops are heaped in black piles. The flames rising from them look like innumerable fiery tongues of black serpents. The road is strewn with bricks, debris and burnt scrap. Where are the residents of this locality? In the middle of the afternoon the road is completely deserted.

'We should head back,' says Mansinghbhai; there is fear in his voice. A funeral-like silence prevails everywhere, except for the grating sound of khachkhach…khachkhach that the tyres of my own ambassador were making. Despite the experience of last night, I do not remember the car making this kind of a sound.

'We keep going straight now,' Madhavsinhbhai says.

Is there a difference in going forwards or backwards? Was it a mistake to set out in this manner with the children?

I turn to the right near Bhulabhai Park. We see Lord Shiva's wrathful *tandava*, the dance of destruction. Shops are turning to ashes before our very eyes. Every single thing in the *kabadi* bazar (scrap market) is on fire. Not a soul in sight that even attempts to extinguish the fires. The children peer out to see if there is a fire engine in sight. 'Property worth lakhs has gone up in smoke.' Mansinghbhai's words. He had two decades' worth of experience trading in scrap, iron and metal parts. He would surely know what he is talking about. It is 2 pm now. Everything has been burning for hours and is likely to continue burning.

We move ahead in silence. We must have barely navigated a kilometre or so. At the crossroad of Behrampura we see a calm, unhurried and listless police station and three or four policemen guarding it. The burning kabadi bazar is right across the police station, its flames leaping sky-high, forming clouds of smoke that were visible to us even from Ellisbridge, three kilometres away. Passing through Sardar Bridge, Paldi and then Panchvati, at last our car arrives at Akil Villa in Swastik Society. Stupefied, we enter our home wordlessly.

As we come in, Parvati, who helps Pratima with the cooking, mentions that, 'Saheb (Jhinabhai Desai 'Sneharashmi') had phoned. He was very upset to learn that you were not at home.'

I dial 8420. The phone rings. It is picked up, and before I can even say hello, I hear, 'Hamid, I told you not to stir out of the house!'

'It was a grave mistake. I apologise,' I humbly say.

'That was not wise. Don't do it again.' Saheb is pacified. His voice is moist. 'I want all of you to come to my house.' His anger had given way to concern and love. Two sides of the same coin.

I relate to him the conditions we had witnessed. He again insists that all of us go over to his house and adds, 'Here, Vijaya wants to talk to you.'

Vijayaben, Jhinabhai's wife, repeats on the phone, 'Hamidbhai, all of you please come over.' Her words come from a place of deep affection. She wants to talk to Pratima. I hand over the phone to Pratima, who expresses her gratitude but makes no commitment. '*Joyinshu*. We will see,' she says, and gently puts the phone back in its cradle.

A vignette from the past flashes before my eyes. It was the annual day celebration in our school Vidyavihar. Among other competitions, there was one that involved playing with flaming torches, like fencing. In the falling darkness of evening, the game created streaks of red, blue and orange, which then formed myriad shapes. Suddenly a swirling, flaming torch slipped out of someone's grasp and flew across towards our end of the room. I was sitting next to Vijayaben when the flaming lathi fell near her. My presence of mind came to the rescue and a couple of us immediately turned a mattress into a ball and put out the fire. My hands were singed in the process, which I didn't realise then. Now, twenty-five years later, Vijayaben's words are trying to put out the fires. She is anxious about our family. The elderly couple has, through a phone conversation, touched our hearts. Our eyes are misty.

Meanwhile, a purposeful ambassador drives into the porch of our bungalow. Surabhai Bharwad, Ratnabhai and Rambhai have arrived.

Surabhai walks in. 'The atmosphere is very bad. Do not go out of the house.'

'Absolutely not. Jhinabhai has also been saying the same thing since last night. Don't worry, we will follow your advice.'

Surabhai sat down for a while, offered words of caution and courage. Then he got ready to leave. As he walked back slowly towards his car, lines of worry were etched visibly on his face and his eyes appeared to look far into the future.

Then Narayanbhai arrives on his bicycle. Narayanbhai, who lives in the slums of Gulbai Tekra, is one of my clients. He had requested me to handle the case of his disputed home property. I am in no state of mind to discuss the details of his case. Nonetheless, I open the office and offer him a seat.

His demeanour and bearing look different. He looks around cautiously and then speaks to me.

'Saheb, listen to this poor man. What I have seen today is a sheer flood, nothing less than a flood! It was terrifying! I have kept twelve of my men ready. They will sleep here in the compound of this bungalow. They will guard the house,' Narayanbhai beseeches, his voice choked with emotion.

I too suspect what he fears, but I hear myself saying, 'Oh no. Nothing is going to happen here. You don't worry about it.' I thank him sincerely and reassure him that I would let him know if I needed anything.

'I will come again, Saheb.' With this, Narayanbhai leaves.

I see Madhavsinhbhai driving into the compound. Sitting next to him is Waheedbhai's eldest daughter Naseem. In the rear seat are Laila and her younger daughter Meena. The car pulls in. I am at the gate of the house.

'Bhai, we have locked up our house,' Laila says as she gets down from the car.

At 3 pm, a green car arrives carrying Kureshibhai, my father. All of us at home and at the Gandhi Ashram call him Abba. He asks after our well-being, sits briefly and leaves.

At about 5 pm we are all sitting around the dining table. Despite trying, we find it difficult to talk. We sip our tea in silence and get up.

Surabhai returns. Just then the telephone in the living room rings. It is Jhinabhai. 'The situation has deteriorated. All of you must come over right away. Arrangements have been made,' he commands.

I respond, 'Saheb, we will have to face the situation. The attachment to property is well and truly gone after seeing so much turn to ashes in seconds. We are preparing to shed our attachment towards life as well.'

'Why? Is life so cheap? Do you want to jump into the fire now? Regardless of how you feel, send Pratima and the children over. I am heading that way.'

Surabhai stays for another ten minutes or so. He has come from the city. He relates to us more incidents. 'I will return again at night,' he says and leaves. Just then another car drives into the compound. It is Mohanbhai from Gandhi Ashram.

Mohan Patel is Abba's trusted secretary, and like a member of the family through the bonds of affection he shares with us. When I see him coming, I say to Madhavsinhbhai, 'Abba seems to have sent him to take us to the Ashram.' But Mohanbhai looks quite shaken. His face is sad and anxious. He doesn't look like he has come to pick us up.

He collapses into the chair next to mine. 'Hamidbhai, our house Imam Manzil at the Gandhi Ashram has been attacked.'

'What...!' Madhavsinhbhai is shocked.

Mohanbhai continues, 'Yes, the crowd turned up twice. They pelted stones and broke the roof tiles. Then they brought down the fence in the front yard with axes. This was around 4.30 pm. Everyone at the Ashram rushed to the spot. They challenged the attacking mob. They tried to reason with them. The mob has dispersed for now, but threatened to return. Sultanaben sent me. I just drove down directly. I have not even bothered to tell Kureshibhai. All of you come with me to my bungalow in Panchsheel.'

Madhavsinhbhai is lost in thought. Then he says, 'Let's go to my house.'

I am thinking if the Imam Manzil in Gandhi Ashram is not safe, then where could I and my family possibly seek shelter? I feel lost. I shut my eyes.

Madhavsinhbhai tries to telephone but is not able to. 'Looks like the phone has also been tampered with,' he says and rushes across to H. M. Desai's house to make a call.

The attack on Imam Manzil has thrown him off kilter. I too am shaken by it. I grew up at the Ashram. Dandi March; arrests at the Ashram, Imam Saheb's sad departure; Ameenama and Kureshibhai's arrests; the Satyagraha; the 1942 Quit India movement and my own participation in it at the age of sixteen;

the imprisonment that followed in Yerwada prison—all these unfold before my eyes like a film reel. Madhavsinhbhai has also been staying at the Ashram since 1945. In the formation of Gujarat as a linguistic state in 1960, it was the Ashram that served as the auspices for the swearing in ceremony of the first Cabinet of Ministers.

I say to Mohanbhai, 'From my birth to adulthood, I have been at the Gandhi Ashram. Our parents married each other at the Ashram. That wedding invitation, *kankotri*, had been sent out on behalf of Gandhiji with his signature.'

Narayanbhai returns. His men ask my permission to organise themselves and guard our bungalow. I express my gratitude and tell them not to undertake any such hardship.

Time goes by. Madhavsinhbhai returns from the bungalow across. 'I phoned to request Hitubhai (Hitendra Desai, Chief Minister of Gujarat) to arrange for armed policemen at Gandhi Ashram. There is a cabinet meeting going on. So I could not talk to Hitubhai. So I tried to contact his personal assistant Mr. Brahmabhatt, but didn't succeed. Finally I made Brahmabhatt's daughter write down this urgent message for Hitubhai and asked her to convey it. I have also requested the Governor's Deputy Mr. Rathod to urgently send a police force to the Ashram. And also to this house in Swastik Society. It needs to be under police protection, I told them.'

'All of you just come to my place. Consider the Panchsheel as entirely your own. It is well-equipped,' Mohanbhai urges again. 'You will like it there, and it is safe as well,' he adds.

I am overwhelmed by such generosity and affection. I compose myself and say, 'Gandhiji's Ashram has been attacked. No place is safe now. Wherever we go, we risk the safety of others. Whatever will be will be. Just as long as all of us are together. I don't expect this house to be safe anymore. It may even explode.'

A black fiat pulls in outside the bungalow. Jhinabhai gets down, looking grave. He quietly walks into the living room and sits down. I tell him about the attack on Imam Manzil. Jhinabhai is speechless with shock. 'I have come to pick you up. Let us go over to my house.' He is extremely insistent and emotional. I see him wipe tears rolling down behind his spectacles with a trembling finger. A poet is wounded.

I so want to express my gratitude to him, but my voice is choked. I try to talk about the overall situation and find my voice. Jhinabhai seems to understand. He is keen to take us to his house, but he understands when I explain. He is pacified when I tell him that Pratima, Laila and the children will go to the Ashram.

We make preparations to send everyone to the Ashram. I want to move the legal papers and briefs. I tell Munna, 'Go climb into the loft. Get gunny sacks from there. I want to put all my legal papers in them.' Munna attaches a ladder to the loft and climbs up.

Madhavsinhbhai says to me, 'There is no need to get this anxious. I have faith that none of the things you are imagining will happen. I understand that wickedness is worrying, but goodness is also reassuring, right?'

I don't argue with him but simply say, 'Madhavsinhbhai, while trusting human goodness is necessary, so is being cautious against evil, don't you think? I am worried about the briefs.'

'I will take them to my house. Don't worry,' he says.

I can see the omens now. Hazy and indistinct, my house seems to be encircled by walls of fire.

First Pratima and the children, then the legal papers, then the house—God knows how such clarity of purpose and priorities came to me! Adverse circumstances do make the mind sharp! I look at the children, at Pratima and Laila. Such complete trust on their faces! Innocent faces hiding their fears, fears they have never before experienced. How much has happened in such a short time. We are all left speechless. My mind struggles to measure the gravity of the situation. Mind, heart, memory, *sanskar*—all work overtime, propelling light and action. The next moment all go numb. Only to revive once again. Such strange experiences these are, like darkness and light alternating each other. Somewhat like a thousand-volt bulb going out of action. Someone turns off the switch, and all objects associated with light go into a passive mode. The very next moment the lights are back on, and everything works overtime! The burden on the mind has certainly increased manifold!

The door connecting the living room and dining room is open. So are the windows in the living room and kitchen. I see Bako going into the kitchen; he has empty ink bottles in his hand. He is fidgeting with something at the window sill, lost in his own world. What goes on in his little mind? What stories lie in his heart? I neither have the time to ask him, nor the courage to know.

Munna (Muneer) who is older than Bako, Aabid (my eldest son, whom we call Baabo), my daughter Kali (Yasmin), and her cousin Naseem (Waheedbhai's daughter)—all of them seem to be wandering about restlessly from one room to another.

Pratima and Laila are sitting quietly across each other at the dining table. They are not voicing their thoughts and fears, not making each other sit up anxiously. They are quiet.

Mohanbhai, Madhavsinhbhai, Jhinabhai and I are in the living room. We look at each other occasionally, and look away.

Finally, we come to a decision. The women and the children would be sent to Gandhi Ashram. No place seems safe. It is good to keep the flock together in times of adversity.

I am not able to think any further. Although we have decided to send everyone to the Ashram, we hesitate to act upon it.

'*Chalo*, Madhavsinhbhai, let's go to the Ashram,' I say. 'Mohanbhai, you stay here.' With this, we take leave of Jhinabhai and Mohanbhai and drive out of Akil Villa.

'We will make arrangements for the legal briefs to be sent away once we come back,' Madhavsinhbhai says.

My car is heading towards the Ashram. It is now 7 pm. Despite the imposition of curfew, there are more people on the streets than usual. Why does the atmosphere look so tense?

We reach the Ashram and meet Kureshibhai. He looks calm and composed. His eyes look especially bright.

'Hello beta, how are things?' Abba asks me.

Madhavsinhbhai and I ask him about updates of the Ashram. Abba tells us:

'A large mob turned up. They pelted stones. We had shut the doors. Only your sister Sultana and Shamim were home. The mob wanted to set the house on fire. I got the news while I was at the office close by. I immediately reached home. Men, women, children, young and old, everyone turned up to rescue Imam Manzil. They pushed the mob back. Despite a shower of stones, people stood unmoving, including Chhaganbhai Joshi, Mansinghbhai and many other men and women. Seeing me come, the girls wouldn't let me go anywhere near the mob. 'Baapa, you don't go!' they said. The Ashram people saved us and the house. The mob dispersed after 4 pm. But it turned up again in another thirty minutes or so. By that time almost every Ashramite was here. They faced the mob, begged them and made them turn away. Before leaving, the troublemakers said, "We will set Imam Manzil ablaze at night, you just wait." We must be thankful to Merciful Allah, such was the courage of the Ashramites. How are things with you, beta?'

I am overwhelmed at this account, but try to sound composed and say, 'I was thinking of sending the children here. If the Ashram can be invaded, our house in Swastik Society can hardly be considered safe. Mohanbhai, Jhinabhai and Madhavsinhbhai have all been insisting that we go over to their place. But I feel we should all be together in times of danger. We will send the women and children here as soon we reach Swastik.'

My elder sister Sultanaben is standing there. I see Shamim hugging her close. They are both quiet. Their eyes are red from weeping. Two years ago when my mother Ameenama passed away, Shamim had looked the same. I look at her pale face and I see her watching me. I feel a rush of love for my eighteen-year old daughter. Shamim rushes into my arms, and I embrace her and caress her gently. I struggle to be the grandmother she has lost. At the tender age of three, I and Pratima had passed on Shamim's care and responsibility to Sultanaben.

Words of consolation choke in my throat. I am not able to console my young daughter. Shamim understands. She presses my hand in hers and kisses it. Then she moves away and stands aside. I see death hovering around us. How do I take this child under my wings? How do I push away the clouds of destruction hovering over her head?

For the first time in the forty-two years of my life, I experience such helplessness.

Sultanaben says, 'Hamidbhai, when Ameenama passed away two years ago, all the Ashramites had come to our house. How many of them came! Similarly today every single man, woman and child from every home associated with the Ashram turned up. They saved us and our home from the mob. They showed such courage. Abba was in his office. Only Shamim and I were home—alone. Poor Shamim was trembling with fear. Yesterday when she was returning home from college, the bus she had taken was not allowed to pull over at the bus stand. The bus began to race ahead. Shamim and her friend, poor things, kept ringing the bell and yelling, 'Please stop the bus! Please…!' and yet the driver continued to race ahead. It went past two bus stands and it is only on the third stand at Keshavnagar that Shamim and her friend finally managed to get down. They had to walk quite a distance from there to reach home. She has been shuddering ever since. But after witnessing the courage of the Ashramites today, she has gained some semblance of strength.'

Mansinghbhai is showing us the Mangalore tiles at the Imam Manzil. Many are broken. The hinges of the verandah door have come off. Axe marks are clear on the entrance gate. The compound is littered with bricks and stones. Mansinghbhai says, 'In the midst of this shower of bricks, Chhaganbhai stood there, begging them to stop with his hands folded.'

My attention is drawn to the entrance of Imam Manzil, especially to the names engraved in English and Hindi on marble blocks. Even those seem to have been tainted by the attacks. To have attacked Gandhi Ashram—the monument emblematic of communal harmony, created by none other than Gandhiji himself! Do they even *know* what they are doing?

I ask Abba, trying not to sound anxious, 'Any arrangements for police protection?' Abba says, 'No arrangements. But the honourable Governor sent his secretary Nanavati with his car to fetch us and give us refuge at the Rajya Bhawan. I expressed my gratitude to the Governor and told him that if I cannot be safe in the Ashram, how can I be safe anywhere else? How do I leave this sacred place? And beta, whatever happens can happen here for all I care. As Khuda wishes. You quickly go and bring Pratima, Laila and the children.'

'Madhavsinhbhai made many phone calls to the police and to Hitubhai while we were at Swastik. Once we go back we will make some more calls,' I tell Abba.

We get back into the car. We go over the Chandrabhaga bridge. When we had passed by the same spot near Vadaj earlier, it was clean. Now there was something burning—in the middle of the road. Madhavsinhbhai straightens himself up. As we go closer we see a cot, a mattress and some clothes on fire, sparks flying out of them. We slow down. Right outside the Vadaj police station, a poor man's property has been set ablaze. None of this was there even an hour ago when we were going to the Ashram. We see three or four policemen coming this side on their cycles. Everything looked like business as usual. The police arrived, as usual, after the burning had taken place. Leisurely. As if they were out on a stroll. Mobsters were marching in from another direction. I see a Vadaj police van parked, and several 'puppets' surrounding it. No action, no movement, nothing. Was the police van for real? I grew restless.

I begin to have premonitions. Is this mob headed towards the Ashram? I hear myself asking Madhavsinhbhai, 'We have decided to send everyone to Gandhi Ashram. But will we be able to negotiate this?' What should we do? I am groping in the dark.

Driving at great speed we manage to reach Swastik Society. There were more and more hordes along the way.

Surabhai also arrives in his car. We try convincing Pratima and Laila to go to the Ashram along with the children. Neither of them would budge. Half an hour goes by. The clock strikes eight. With a heavy heart we put the children into the car.

Bako steals up to Madhavsinhbhai, pulls at his kurta sleeve and says, 'Kaka, if our house is attacked and the lights are blown off, I have kept four kerosene lamps at the window sill in the kitchen. I couldn't find a torch, so I have filled up diyas with kerosene and put wicks in them. They will be useful to you, okay, when all the lights are gone. And keep this matchbox with you.' He slips the matchbox into Madhavsinh's pocket and runs back to his mother in the car.

Surabhai says, 'Hamidbhai, don't worry about anything. I will make sure they reach the Ashram safely.'

With Surabhai's car leading in front and the children in Mohanbhai's car following him, all head towards the Ashram. Surabhai is with them. Otherwise I wouldn't have the courage to send the children.

Every minute is sliding away.

There are three chairs in the lawn of our bungalow. I, Madhavsinhbhai and Muljibhai, who has just arrived to check on me, are sitting together and talking about the events unfolding around us. It is almost half past eight. The moon has risen. The gentle moonlight, a cool breeze and a moist lawn provide some relief to the restless and tensed mind.

I look up at the bungalow and say to Madhavsinhbhai, 'Why are we still here—so we can safeguard this property? And what of our near and dear ones? From seventy-year old Abba to nine-year old Bako, everyone is at the Ashram. We don't yet know whether the children reached safely or not. Not to mention the clouds of fear that hover over the Ashram. Chalo, let's go there and see.'

Madhavsinhbhai says, 'Just what I was also thinking, Hamidbhai. Yes, let's go. Once we come back from the Ashram, I will move all the briefs to my house.'

The three of us get into the car. The car moves slowly. It passes by the stadium and Sardar Patel Colony, goes through Panchsheel Society to Shantinagar, and eventually arrives at Ashram Road. There are hordes of people there.

At Ashram Road a crowd of over hundred people gherao the car. Lathis, pipes and iron rods in their hands, people with fearsome faces and raging eyes—it was like facing a gigantic demon carved out of over hundred or two hundred people. This is the first time I am witnessing a scene like this. It is unbelievable. I am almost in denial. The sanskaras of peace refuse to let me take cognizance of this reality. Is this real or a nightmare? My mind goes blank. There is only darkness. Yet once again there is illumination, and a thousand lamps light up.

The mob stops the car. A bunch of people encircle us. Muljibhai shouts, 'It is us, do you see, it is *us* people! We have to go to Sabarmati!'

Perhaps there is still some semblance of respect for our white khadi clothes, and Muljibhai's age, for our car is allowed to pass. We pass by several such hordes, and each time what follows is the same question, the same answer, the same ritual. The car moves on towards Vadaj. There is a huge crowd at the Vadaj corner, at least a thousand people or more. I say to Madhavsinhbhai, 'This is impossible to negotiate. I am sure someone or the other, a client or perhaps a student from this crowd would recognise me. And if he says, "Oh this is Kureshi Saheb," what will happen then? I don't think we can go to the Ashram through this. It is impossible now to even turn back. In fact that will draw suspicion.'

We could neither move forward nor go back. In a wink my mind took a decision: turn left towards Nava Vadaj. That was the only option left. I turned the car gently towards the low-lying region of Nava Vadaj. From the rear seat Muljibhai sounded caution, 'Saheb, keep the dipper on.'

As the car moved ahead, as far as the eyes could see, by the light of the headlights we saw mobs wielding pipes, lathis and iron rods, littering the skyline with sharp angry spikes. We were now trapped from three sides by angry mobs.

I sat up in my seat. What pleasure this is! My mind is filled with a strange equanimity. Suddenly, I have a flash of inspiration. At the end of this road is Surabhai Bharwad's house. He is a very respected figure in this area. Even children in this area would know him. I address the marching crowd and say, 'Bhai, where is Surabhai's house? That's where we want to go.'

I have a distinct feeling it was not I who was saying these words. A mysterious divine force made me utter them.

'He is a Surabhai acquaintance,' I hear a voice in the crowd say.

The effect is quite magical. The crowd makes way for us to leave. We use the mantra of 'Surabhai' at several places on that long road and finally arrive at Surabhai's house. Now there was no choice but to go to Swastik. We take the kuccha road from Nava Vadaj and speedily reach the railway lines at Panchsheel.

We go via the Sindhi colony. Houses are deserted. A pall of gloom hangs over the entire area. Where are the people?

We pass by the rear side of Gujarat Vidyapith, touching which is the Navjivan Press, and cross the railway tracks near Gujarat High Court. We go past the Ambalal Ice-cream place. Swastik Society is to our left. Suddenly, the headlights catch eight or ten young men who seem to be rushing out of Swastik Society. They are rioters, clearly.

'Madhavsinhbhai, our house has been attacked.'

I turn right towards my home, and see a mob of three or four hundred people all over my house.

'Hamidbhai, they will torch the car—reverse it quickly!'

'Hurry, police station,' urges Muljibhai.

Mechanically I reverse the car. I take the route from Navrangpura village and park my car at the Navrangpura police station. Madhavsinhbhai and I rush inside.

I introduce myself to the officer-in-charge. 'This is Madhavsinhbhai, Ex-Deputy Minister, Home Department. Once he gives you the details, please do the needful.'

Madhavsinhbhai adds, 'Hamidbhai Kureshi's bungalow in Swastik Society has been attacked and they will torch it any moment. We just saw that and rushed here. Please send a police van immediately.'

The police officer replied, 'At Kureshibhai's house? Vyas Saheb has already taken a van near Mirambika Hotel.'

'Madhavsinhbhai, *khalaas*! It's all over! They have burned Waheedbhai's house as well. My brother's house is right next to Mirambika Hotel. There is nobody at home.'

Madhavsinhbhai tells the officer, 'The same thing will happen to Hamidbhai's house if you don't do something immediately.'

A police van stood outside the police station. There were a few lathi-carrying policemen who moved about aimlessly. The telephone keeps ringing. I hear an officer say, 'A Mujawar has been killed near the river bank. A murder complaint is being filed.'

Ten, fifteen, twenty, almost twenty-five minutes go by. The police officer is still struggling to send a van over to my house. There is only one van and very few policemen. None of them seem armed. There are constant phone calls asking for help. The flustered police officers are losing their temper and patience. The van, the police, us—everything is stationary. Only the minutes tick on relentlessly.

The policemen begin to climb into the van, chatting and joking, as if they were going on an excursion. They all occupy the van, but there is no sign of the driver. The van continues to be stationary. I hear the cops chatting amongst themselves:

'The driver has gone to have chai. He will come.'

'He was here a moment ago.'

A search is launched to find the driver.

A police jeep pulls over behind the van. Someone says, 'It is D.I.G. Saheb.'

We introduce ourselves and quickly give him an overview of the situation.

D.I.G. Malia looks confused and irritated. He knows Madhavsinhbhai. Madhavsinhbhai urges him to come with us.

The D.I.G.'s words betray exasperation, 'My duty is of a different kind. I am not in charge of this job. But all right, chalo.' He agrees to join us. Madhavsinhbhai sits next to him in the jeep.

But how do we move? Where is the driver of the van ahead of us? My patience is wearing thin. At last, the driver ambles along leisurely. He occupies his designated seat with flair, like a traveler out on a sightseeing tour. The van stutters into life as he presses the ignition key, but shows no sign of moving. The policemen get down to push the van, and finally it takes off.

A police officer commands the van driver to stay behind the jeep. The jeep moves ahead, followed by the van—there is no coordination whatsoever between the two vehicles as they leave. Will they ever reach on time, these two?

I go to my car parked outside the police station and get in. Muljibhai sits next to me wordlessly.

My attachment to my house seems to be slipping away like pearls from a broken necklace. I had bought a beautiful miniature of the Meenakshi Temple and fastidiously taken care of it; it was always on my table. Will that too be gone? Will the rioters break that little temple? I hope they neither burn it nor destroy it. I hope they take it to someone's home and install it as a temple.

And what of the legal briefs? I had seen rioters at my house through the headlights of my car. I hope the educated ones among them would at least cast an eye on the titles of the briefs; along with my name, the name Madhavsinh Solanki also appears there. The case file of Shri Gopal Temple at Pansora is right on top of the pile; I had prepared the case for it just yesterday. There are numerous other briefs as well—the Khodiyar Mata Temple and other temple trusts. If only...if only a literate person's eyes fall on them, they would all be saved. So many fortunes and lives rest upon those legal papers. If only Madhavsinhbhai and the police reach on time, they would all be saved.... But worry gnaws at me constantly, and terrible premonitions prevail.

The copies of *Raghuvansh* and *Kumarsambhav* that Pratima had enthusiastically bought, along with gifted copies of Vinoba

Bhave's *Quransaar* and the *Bhagvadgita* flash before my eyes. Omar Khayyam, Confucius, Shakespeare, Bernard Shaw, Khalil Gibran, Byron, Keats, Ghalib, Tulsidas, Meera, Kabir, Iqbal, Tagore, Buddha, Mahavir, Jesus Christ, Gandhiji—will all of them be lit up in one huge pyre?

I am thinking particularly of Confucius and Buddha. These two radiant stars, these guiding lights of the sixth century before the common era—one in China and the other a gazillion miles away in India—both lived around the same time. They sat side by side on my bookshelf. Will they also burn together?

I look at the seconds and minutes slipping away on my wrist watch as myriad thoughts and memories whirl around in my head. So many things come back, so many are forgotten. Strange emotions. Aabid, Munno, Bako, Kali, Pratima—I see all of them before my very eyes. Pratima is standing right next to me, with little Shamim hugging her close.

Just then an ambassador rushes into the police station compound, breaking my reverie. Surabhai climbs out of it, accompanied by Dahyabhai Nayak and Chhaganbhai Joshi. 'Hamidbhai, come, let's go! Madhavsinhbhai is calling for you,' Surabhai says, adding, 'We are coming from Swastik Society.'

I hand over my car to Muljibhai and tell him, 'Now you take care of this.' I go and sit next to Surabhai in their car.

On the way Surabhai asks me, 'Did you go from Vadaj to Nava Vadaj?' I say yes. He continues, 'You took a turn at the end of the road, and just then, right behind you, a murder took place. The mobs killed someone.' Our car moves ahead. There are some twenty-five policemen, rather khaki puppets, standing there.

All our neighbours have gathered at Akil Villa, our home in Swastik Society. Some are carrying torches. As I get down from the car, I am encircled by many arms. Ushaben, Piyushbhai and others are using their torches and giving me an account of things.

I see columns of smoke rising from my office. All the tubelights and bulbs have been destroyed; the wires have been burnt. Books, briefs, papers, files, documents—everything is burnt. I see a half-torn cover of India's Constitution. The Constitution itself is burnt.

Splinters of glass from broken windows lie scattered everywhere. Both drawers of my table have been emptied and torched. The godrej cupboard containing my legal documents is empty and burnt black. The blades of the ceiling fan are grotesquely misshapen, twisted and burnt. The walls, doors, windows—all are burnt black and turned to char.

The sofas, chairs and cabinets from the living room have been dragged into the dining room and put next to each other. The radio lies on the floor, smashed to smithereens. The telephone is broken, the telephone wires charred. The carpet is burnt.

The row of gleaming steel thalis, katoris and utensils in the kitchen is gone. All utensils are gone. The kitchen almirahs are empty. The dining room chairs lie in a pile as broken, burnt pieces of wood. The dining table is littered with sundry things from the kitchen. The refrigerator door is flung wide open and the contents of the fridge lie strewn about. The floor is littered with pieces of glass and spilled liquid. My heart is in turmoil.

The previous year Pratima was gravely ill and bedridden, counting her last breaths. Vaid Govindprasad was summoned, and he had come home. He saw her condition and asked us to arrange for oxygen, which we did immediately. We moved Pratima to the Civil Hospital. But the oxygen cylinder there proved to be of no use; the narrow, compressed air pipe would not allow the oxygen to reach her lungs. Unless the lungs had ventilation there was no possibility of saving her life. Helpless, we stood watching as Pratima lay gasping for breath—it was unbearable to see her. She longed for a quick release. Just then Dr. O. P. Gupta arrived. He examined the patient intently. Five, ten, fifteen minutes passed, or an eternity. He finished his examination, took a piece of paper and wrote down the name of an injection. 'It is difficult to procure,' he said, 'But try. It is absolutely essential for her survival.'

A.C.T.H. injections were rarely available those days. We went around all the medical stores. One of them had two reserved for another patient. The shopkeeper advised us, 'Go to Teen Darwaja. If you get it there, well and good; if not I will give them to you.' We went to all the chemists at Teen Darwaja. There at last, in a store at Pankor Naka, we found a stock of eight injections. We bought all eight—that was the entire stock of A.C.T.H. injections in the city of Ahmedabad.

Hospitals have scant records of the usage of A.C.T.H. injections. It is believed that the slightest error in administering it can lead to a fatality. Dr. Gupta's decision to administer this injection was both courageous and extremely risky. Pratima's sister Hansa was a house doctor at the Civil Hospital those days. She was busy nursing Pratima. She took me aside and said, 'Only Dr. Gupta could have taken this decision. It is like walking on a razor's edge. His prognosis is always accurate. Otherwise, no one would dare recommend this injection.'

The injection arrived and was administered. Another one followed. Gradually, her breathing was restored; the patient's face assumed life again.

Dr. Gupta had dropped by. A smile broke out on his face as he said to Madhavsinhbhai, 'The injection has worked. Really, I didn't know what to do. There was a fifty per cent chance of failure.'

After about a month or so, Pratima recovered fully and was discharged from the hospital. When we were thanking Dr. Gupta and saying our goodbyes to him, he had told us, 'The injections you have not used do keep them carefully. You never know when you might need them again.' We had carefully stored these life-giving vials in our refrigerator. Today they lie as pieces of broken glass and spilt liquid.

My mind and heart are engulfed by grief. I don't have the courage to see anything more. I don't have the desire to estimate the measure of loot, arson and robbery. I feel as if these goods and property were never mine. That none of it belonged to me in the first place. But it is the destruction of the legal briefs that upsets me more, and I tremble with helplessness and rage. Those papers were testimonies to the struggles of those seeking justice. I am anxious about the fates of those people.

I step into our bedroom, only to step out just as quickly—it is filled with thick black smoke.

The compound is packed with neighbours who have rushed in. Piyushbhai Gandhi says, 'Before the mob descended upon your house, your maid Kamu and her husband Kaluji had come running to warn us. Poor people, they were both out of breath. And barely five minutes thereafter, a mob of three or four hundred turned up. They had petrol cans, kerosene bottles, sticks, pipes and stones with them. I tried to dissuade them. Dr. Pushpendra Bhatt had also come running. There were others as well. We all shouted and pleaded and begged them to stop. The ones at the forefront looked hesitant initially. But by then the mob at the rear had already broken into the house from another entrance. Someone dealt a blow to Dr. Bhatt and he started bleeding from the head. It was best to move away, we felt. We were only four or five of us, empty-handed, facing an armed horde of over four hundred people. They destroyed and burnt down everything, Hamidbhai.'

Ushaben, Savitri, Jayshree and other neighbours are busy trying to extinguish the fires, clearing the debris and rearranging the house. Even an ill-disposed Rashmiben is busy helping.

The faujdar comes up to me and says, 'Saheb, so you are here finally. Let's lock up the bungalow. We are leaving now.'

'I had locked it up. But there is no need to do so anymore,' I tell him.

The faujdar is in haste. There is a possibility the mob might return to the spot. Madhavsinhbhai suggests posting some policemen for security.

'We don't have extra men,' says the faujdar. He leaves with all the policemen by the van. Perhaps they had similar jobs to attend to elsewhere.

Now I am only thinking of the Ashram. 'Madhavsinhbhai, let's go to Gandhi Ashram.'

'You go on ahead. I will stay here,' he says, refusing to leave Akil Villa. His hands are moving blindly through the burnt remains of books, papers, pieces of glass. As his fingers brush against a shard of glass, I see drops of blood fall, but he doesn't seem to notice. His kurta, dhoti and koti have soot on them.

'Madhavsinhbhai, please let us go,' I urge him. 'Let all this be now.'

'No, Hamidbhai. I will stay here. All this has to be rearranged. The fire has been extinguished at the top, but there are embers still burning inside.'

Surabhai intervenes, 'Let Madhavsinhbhai be. Hamidbhai, let us go.'

I sit in Surabhai's car, flanked by Dahyabhai on one side and Surabhai on the other. Chhaganbhai has also joined us. 'Let's also stop by Waheedbhai's house on the way,' I suggest.

The car pulls over outside Waheedbhai's house. The house is fully lit. The doors and windows are wide open. A pile of household objects is burning in the compound. We get off the car. As we walk into the compound, neighbours come and give us an account of what happened. They are very anxious and ask us to leave immediately. 'The rioters will come back if they see you. We had phoned the police and even sent people on bicycles to call them, but in vain. The property documents still show this house as belonging to Bhanubhai Thakker. Hence it is still standing.'

'After everything was burnt and over, a police van came by and left,' someone says.

I am startled by a moaning sound. I look up. At seventy-five, Chhaganbhai can no longer take the mindless brutality of what he was witnessing. He is moaning and whimpering like a child. Though it is I who needed to be reassured, I found myself trying to reassure him instead. 'Is this what we have been living for? To see *this*...?' Chhaganbhai said disconsolately. For someone who had undertaken the Dandi March and accompanied Gandhi on most journeys, this was more than he could bear.

About two years ago, when my mother Ameenama died at the age of seventy-two, I was inconsolable and particularly remorseful about her premature death. Today, I am relieved that she did not live to witness this. How would she have endured this bestiality?

Everything in Waheedbhai's house has been destroyed. All that is left is a picture hanging on the wall—of Gandhiji lost in prayer. On Gandhiji's birth anniversary, little Shamim had lovingly got four such photographs framed. One of them was given to Waheedbhai. Someone has run a rod through the glass frame and shattered it. A hole is visible in Gandhiji's heart; his body is torn, but his face is still lost in prayer. Amidst all this wreckage, we notice that Laila's favourite Sai Baba statue stands intact. It has a garland around it. No one has touched the statue. We get back into the car.

The jeep races towards Imam Manzil via Ashram Road. I tell Surabhai, 'The situation has deteriorated. It is best to make a dignified exit before any more disasters strike us. Yesterday they torched shops and godowns; today it is homes and residences. Tomorrow it may be human life. The government and the police seem unable to do anything to stop them. Just look at our city today! It has been handed over to a mob of destroyers. Surabhai, we have lived with our heads held high all these years. Are we going to die now—and *how*? I would prefer if all of us, starting from Abba in Imam Manzil to little Bako, take potassium cyanide…' Surabhai does not let me finish and tells me not to entertain such thoughts. 'I am not saying this out of despair or sentimentalism,' I tell him, 'But this seems to me to be the only sensible path left.' Surabhai's eyes moisten.

At Vadaj we see the same mobs, the same weapons. Surabhai's is a well-recognised car. No one stops us. We manage to reach the Ashram unharmed.

The atmosphere at Imam Manzil is charged. The entire Ashram is on its toes. Dahyabhai Nayak who must be in his seventies at least, the elderly Dilkhushbhai Diwanji, Dattubhai, Pratapbhai, Khimjibhai, Ishwarbhai Amin, Dr. Trivedi, Kishanbhai, Kanubhai Vaghela, the physically challenged and elderly Ramjibhai Badiya, Mansinghbhai, Anil Patel, Mohanbhai—all of them are present, and they all look poised. There are younger people and children in the Ashram too, at least a hundred and fifty in number; they have also gathered in the compound of Imam Manzil.

It is twelve in the night. Screams and cries can be heard from neighbouring Vadaj, from Ranip, from all sides. As soon as we get down from the jeep, we are asked, 'They burnt down your house? And Waheedbhai's as well?' So the news had already reached the Ashram. How does news travel so fast, I wondered, mystified.

My eyes search for Kureshibhai, but he is nowhere to be seen.

Sultanaben comes up to me. I ask her, 'Where is Abba?'

Mohanbhai replies, 'Abba is sleeping inside.'

Astonished, I say, 'How is he able to sleep amidst so much tension and chaos?'

'That is the sign of his faith in God,' someone replies.

Mohanbhai goes inside the house and wakes up Kureshibhai. He comes out rubbing his eyes. There is exhaustion on his face, but no sign of fear or distress. His steps are slow and measured. Abba puts his hand on my shoulder and says, 'Beta, how are you?'

'Abba, they have burnt my house. Bhai's furniture has been thrown out and torched. They have robbed clothes, utensils, everything.'

'*Khuda ko jo manzoor thha* [As God willed it],' says Abba, his hand caressing my head. He walks towards the living room with measured steps and sits down on a cot.

I look at all the people standing in the compound of Imam Manzil. They have all braced themselves to be the guardians of Imam Manzil. They are determined to ward off any attack on our house. I see well-built Bharwad youth as well. I don't know them.

Anil Patel mentions, 'Surabhai has brought them here for help. From Nava Vadaj.' They are all alert and attentive—Surabhai, Navalbhai, Mansinghbhai.

Behind us, from the direction of Vadaj and Chandrabhaga, screams and wails are heard. There must be a mob of at least five hundred people. We hear sounds from the direction of Ranip as well.

Someone mentions that Pratima and the children are with Pratima's mother Shardaben. I go over there. I wake up Pratima and tell her everything. She is stunned. She doesn't utter a word. She is unable to. I sense that she wants to cry. Perhaps she should. But she is fighting back her tears. I come away, leaving a choked Pratima alone. She should get it off her chest, I feel.

I am walking back towards Imam Manzil when I feel someone's presence behind me. I turn around to see—it is Pratima. Together we go to Imam Manzil. Abba is lying on the cot in the living room. Pratima walks up to him, puts her head in his lap and sobs uncontrollably. Abba gently caresses her head. Shamim comes and stands beside them. She cries and hugs her mother. Fighting my own tears, I leave the room. I am glad Pratima could weep.

Surabhai is standing guard. I tell him, 'The situation is terrible. The mob we saw near Vadaj may come here. You or Navalbhai go to our home in Swastik. Take Madhavsinhbhai with you and go and meet Hitubhai in person. Request him to make arrangements for armed police immediately. Hitubhai may not know the seriousness of the situation here. It is possible that our message on phone did not reach him.'

Surabhai says, 'Yes, I will go.'

Just then an ambassador pulls into the compound at great speed. Surabhai walks up to the car and converses with someone sitting inside. The ambassador goes away equally swiftly.

Meanwhile, one by one I greet everyone outside Imam Manzil. People try to comfort me, give me courage. Today all bodies in the Ashram had but one soul. Not one person intends to sleep or to rest.

Pratima heads back to her mother Shardaben's house. 'Don't worry about the children,' she tells me. 'Abba is also resting.'

My attention is drawn to the neem tree under which Surabhai is giving instructions to two of his Bharwad friends. Before they start the car, I go up to them and ask, 'Surabhai, where is the car headed? Aren't you or Navalbhai going?'

Surabhai instructs the driver to turn off the ignition. He holds my hand and takes me into a corner. Two of his companions also join us. 'Hamidbhai, these Bharwad friends of mine are young and sturdy. They are not worshippers of *ahimsa*. They will not give up without a good fight. Look at them. They are empty-handed. The person in the other car tells us that a large armed mob is headed here from the direction of Vadaj. What do I give these young Bharwads to fight them back? I need to send the car to get arms.'

I am stunned.

One of his companions says, 'Hamidbhai, ahimsa is another name for timidity. Never mind if there is a loss of some lives; we need to have some courage.'

I say, 'Surabhai, to what avail is all this? To protect the Kureshi family and the Imam Manzil? No, this will not be. There will be no one left if we take this path. And the house will also be destroyed. Think of the Gandhi Ashram, Surabhai, and forget all this please. I do not agree with bringing weapons. If something untoward happens, how is Kureshibhai ever going to show his face to the world tomorrow? What face will I show? The Ashram will be in ruins. Please let us ask the Bharwads to leave. You, I and Navalbhai are guarding this front now. My father has gone to sleep in the living room, leaving all his worries to Allah. Should the situation worsen, we will carry him and bring him outside.'

Surabhai is silent. He gestures his men to get down from the jeep.

I continue, 'Surabhai, if you want to take recourse to arms, please wake up Madhavsinhbhai and go to Hitubhai. The state can use its arms to protect us.'

The three of us—Surabhai, Navalbhai and I—join the men who stand encircling the Ashram and Imam Manzil. From all around us, we continue to hear heartrending and frightening screams.

It is past midnight. The ambassador arrives again. Someone gets down; he is clad in khadi clothes and a Gandhi cap. He comes up to us and gives us an account: 'The mob had reached Vadaj, but we stopped them there. I told the mob, "Are you going to the Gandhi Ashram to burn it? Kureshibhai there believes that if God wants the house to be burnt, so be it, and with that faith he has gone to sleep. But in order to protect him and his house Imam Manzil, a hundred or two hundred people—Hindus, people of your own religion—are ready to lay down their lives. Whatever you wish to do will also take the lives of some of your co-religionists. Is that what you want?" When I said this, they stood still. I don't think they will come here now. You can rest assured as far as Vadaj is concerned. Of course Sabarmati and Ranip are still possibilities.'

He continued to give us comfort.

Shantibhai Raval, a family friend for long years, said, 'I was with him. This well-wisher managed to avert the mob.'

Everyone felt relieved and grateful, but their decision to stand guard remained firm.

It is 5 am. I see old Dahyabhai Nayak; he has stood sentinel all night. 'Everyone must keep awake until 6 am,' he says.

Not an iota of sleep all night. But there is no exhaustion, no sleepiness. I manage a shuteye and am back on my feet before six.

It is 7 am. Madhavsinhbhai arrives from Akil Villa. I give him the saga of the previous night and add, 'The night's mob was averted. But what about the day now? And what of the night once again? Why don't you meet Hitubhai in person, please? Perhaps he is not acquainted with the situation here. There is no alternative but to beef up this place with armed security. It is difficult to say what will happen next.'

Madhavsinhbhai agrees with me. He phones Hitubhai for an appointment and leaves for Shahibagh to meet him. Upon his return he tells me, 'I told Hitubhai everything. Inspector General of Police Pavri was also present there. Hitubhai asked me to consult Pavri. Then he especially asked Pavri, "I hope you have heard what Madhavsinhbhai has to say. Send armed guards to the Ashram." Pavri said, "Yes Sir, I will do so immediately."'

We feel much reassured and comforted by the Chief Minister's instructions, the I.G.P.'s promise and Madhavsinhbhai's account. From the way Madhavsinhbhai described the entire meeting and saw its swift developments, we have faith that in another thirty minutes at most armed policemen would be guarding the Ashram.

Should riots take place and people get killed at the Ashram, it could lead to ugly developments. Bloodshed in Gandhiji's own Ashram, and during Gandhiji's centenary year, would bring Ahmedabad, Gujarat and all of India a bad name in the world. However the rioters were cowards; they would run away from guns. So the thought was a comforting one.

Madhavsinhbhai, who remains by my side, tells me, 'On the way back from Hitubhai's, we stopped at Akil Villa. Dhirubhai Desai had also come by. Apparently Babubhai [Babubhai Jashbhai Patel] had dropped him at Swastik Society at around ten in the morning. Dhirubhai had come to know that your house was burnt. He was very upset. He decided to call for a meeting of the members of Swastik Society. The meeting will be held at his daughter Ushaben's house, which is right next to Akil Villa. Dhirubhai is filled with remorse. He has put a cot in the compound of your house, where he has stationed himself to guard your house. He says, "This is where I will be until Hamidbhai comes back with his family." It is too much for him. He has a delicate and frail body, and health complications due to a cardiac history. Everyone is trying hard to dissuade him, but he refuses to move away from your house.'

I make a silent bow to the gentle and affectionate Dhirubhai.

3.30 PM. It is now six hours since Hitubhai's orders and I.G.P. Pavri's assurance. There is no sign of any armed policemen.

Dahyabhai, the administrator at the Ashram, comes over. Madhavsinhbhai says, 'Dahyabhai, despite the Chief Minister's instructions, the police have not turned up. Now just call up the Governor Shrimannarayanji and request him to either make immediate arrangements or come himself. If he makes a personal appearance, it will make an impact. And Shrimannarayanji is also an Ashramite, isn't he? He drops by at the Ashram on so many occasions.'

'Sure.' Dahyabhai leaves.

I am pondering over Madhavsinhbhai's words. He is right. Governor Saheb does visit the Ashram on many occasions. As a child, his wife Madalsaben had played with other children in Imam Manzil. She was a friend of my late mother Ameenama. Her father Jamnalal Bajaj was an inmate of the Ashram, a companion to Gandhi, and also a neighbour of Imam Saheb.

Time goes by. I grow impatient. I say to Madhavsinhbhai, 'We have but a few hours now. Once it is eight o' clock and night falls, nothing will be in our control. Yesterday we knew that the bungalow was going to be torched; yet we could not do anything. Last night some people slept at Shardaben's, Sultanaben and Shamim were at Jayaben's, Kureshibhai was at Imam Manzil, while I simply moved about all night—that is how we survived the night. We hear screams and wails throughout the day. I have no faith that tonight will be a safe night for my family. To become helpless again, and put the entire Ashram community at risk in the process? No, it is better to do what I had suggested to Surabhai.' I tell him the same thing—that all of us in the Kureshi family should simply…

But Madhavsinhbhai does not let me finish either and interrupts me, saying, 'I will try once again. Let me remind Hitubhai of his morning's commitment.'

We go over to Dahyabhai's office to make a phone call. We see Dahyabhai coming from the opposite direction. I ask him, 'Did you get through to the Governor Saheb?'

'Yes, I did,' says Dahyabhai. 'I informed him that we had spoken personally to Hitubhai to provide security to the Ashram, but nothing has been implemented so far. I also requested him if he could make a personal visit. But Governor Saheb said, "I have talked to the Chief Minister for security. However, I have been advised by the I.G.P. not to move out." He expressed his helplessness.'

I am exasperated. What is the I.G.P. up to? He is the one with power over the armed guards. We have made so many desperate pleas for protection. Couldn't he have sent at least four, or even two, armed policemen? And does he have to stop even the Governor from coming to the Ashram?!

Madhavsinhbhai makes one last ditch effort to get in touch with Hitubhai. He gives us an update: 'I told Hitubhai that despite the decision taken at nine this morning, no security has been provided until now when it is nearing four o' clock. When he heard this, Hitubhai said, "What! Nothing has been done so far? Let me talk to Pavri right now." Hitubhai was quite concerned. Anyway, I am going to Akil Villa now.' Madhavsinhbhai left with Surabhai accompanying him.

5.30 PM. Still no sign of police. I enter the living room of Imam Manzil and sit down. My mind is abuzz. How long will I keep troubling Madhavsinhbhai, and everyone else for that matter? I talk to Abba of the ultimate eventuality. 'Abba, we have only a couple of hours left with us. You and I need to decide. The entire city is filled with bloodshed. Day before yesterday, the rioters burnt shops and stores, robbed and ransacked them. Last night, homes and household goods were subjected to the same treatment. I have premonitions that now human lives will be attacked. My house was burnt last night. Waheedbhai's too. We saw the signs of impending disaster beforehand. But we were in denial. So much has been destroyed. My legal briefs have been burnt. I fear it is now going to be our bodies. Abba, you and I have to decide what is to be done now. We will risk the lives of those who protect and shelter us. Imagine what will happen if they lose their lives. Before bringing any harm to their lives, it is far better that all of us bring an end to our own lives with potassium…'

'Hamid beta, what nonsense is this? Have faith in Khuda and be patient.'

'I have faith only in God, Abba. I have no other faith left. The state is weak and passive. It looks as if it will not be providing protection. The police is disobeying the Chief Minister's orders—tell me, how could that even be possible! The police has not arrived. And it will probably not arrive, at least not in time. The minutes are ticking away. Please suggest something. I can only think of the one alternative I have mentioned—it is the only one with dignity in it.'

Abba fell into deep thought. After a while his moist eyes seemed to light up. Perhaps he saw the truth in what I was saying. In a voice that was soft, firm and grave he said to me, 'Beta, it is almost six. It is time for namaaz. Let us talk later.'

He gets up slowly, spreads the mat and begins to pray. Five, ten, twenty, twenty-five minutes go by. Abba rises, folds his mat. Just then Surabhai's car arrives at the entrance of the compound with a police van behind him. Surabhai, Madhavsinhbhai and a few others who had gone to Swastik Society get off the car. One by one, four armed men of the State Reserve Police disembark from the van.

I heave a huge sigh of relief. People surround Madhavsinhbhai. The clouds of terror seem at last to lift and move away.

Madhavsinhbhai comes and stands beside me. 'I met Dhirubhai at Swastik. The meeting is today at 5.30 pm.'

Dahyabhai arrives and addresses everyone, 'Although the police are here, our responsibility is not yet over. We will stand guard tonight as well.' People are alert and ready to take up their posts. Their courage has gone up, and there is no waning of passion either.

How would the rioters have known that the policemen had taken up positions at the Ashram? Suddenly a hush has fallen over that direction. Sounds of violence, wailing and screaming can still be heard in the distance. But their fearsomeness and intensity has begun to wane somewhat.

Night has fallen. It is midnight. The Ashram continues to be guarded and watched. Madhavsinhbhai and I meet small groups in charge of the night patrol. Everyone is awake and alert.

It is morning. At 5.30 am, I go and lie down on my bed briefly. And I am ready and showered by 8.30 am. Madhavsinhbhai is also ready.

Abba says, 'Hamid, we have gone through an ordeal by fire, an *agniparikshа*.'

'Yes, Abba. Not just us, how many people have gone through this trial with us.'

A string of visitors follow. The eminent Dhirubhai Desai arrives, unmistakable in his prominent beard and white khadi clothes. Our long-time neighbour and well-wisher Ushaben Gandhi has accompanied her father. I walk up to them to welcome them. Both father and daughter are in an emotional state.

Dhirubhai takes me into his arms and breaks down as he says, 'Hamidbhai, you had to leave your home...' his frail old body racked with sobs.

I do not know how to comfort him.

Abba comes over. Dhirubhai regains his composure somewhat and says, 'Hamidbhai, your house could not be saved amidst so many houses. I came to know only when I went to Swastik with Babubhai yesterday. I met Dr. Pushpendra Bhatt and told him, "It is our responsibility. Can't we take care of one house of a minority community? I have called a meeting today." Dr. Bhatt said, "Who will come?" I said, "At least you will, won't you? We will have a two-person meeting then. We must do our duty." After scheduling a meeting at 5.30 pm, I circulated the notice to all the bungalows. Not five or ten, but over a hundred people turned up—men, women, young and old. There must be at least sixty women. They all unanimously decided to protect your house. They watched your house all night, men as well as women. You would have been pleased to see their commitment. A beautiful unity has been forged. I am very much at your house. I will leave only once you return, Hamidbhai. Now stop worrying about the house. Swastik Society has re-awakened. The rioters will not dare come there again.'

Dhirubhai's quiet, unassuming strength is spellbinding. He leaves after an hour or so.

'Hansa has come from the Civil Hospital,' Pratima informs me.

Hansa tiptoes into the house. She hugs me and weeps. I make her sit beside me. She speaks haltingly between sobs: 'There are corpses without count at the Civil Hospital, Hamidbhai. The morgue, the basement—everything is choked with dead bodies. There is such scarcity of space that bodies are lying out in the open. Body-parts mutilated, burnt and cut… Even we doctors shudder to look at them. None of us can swallow a morsel. The wounded are in such terrible condition I cannot even describe to you. Among the dead there are also women and little children…' Hansa's face has turned white and stony. Her lips are parched. What she has witnessed has changed her. She is very anxious about her husband Sajjad Hussain, who lives in Vadodara where he is pursuing medicine. I don't know if there is fear or resignation in Hansa's eyes, but what is clearly visible is an overwhelming empathy.

'The entire staff of Civil Hospital is working day and night,' she says.

'Dada is calling you,' someone says. Ravishankar Maharaj has entered the living room. He sits down looking despondent.

I apprise him of the developments. I also tell him about the students.

Maharaj says, 'How could the students do this? It's too much. They stopped my car as well. Made me get down. Once they recognised me, they said, "Ravishankar Maharaj ki jai!" I said, "Are you bringing glory to Mother India by doing this?" They said, "We will hail you, but we will not listen to you today." They have lost their heads, these students.'

Maharaj stays for a while, extends comfort and inspiration, and then leaves. He appears quite upset, also struggling to see what goes behind the rioting mind.

It is about noon. A convoy of cars arrives at Imam Manzil. Governor Shrimannarayanji, Chief Minister Shri Hitubhai Desai and Minister of Construction Shri Babubhai Jashbhai Patel arrive. They all look downcast and anxious. They are also accompanied by the Defence Minister, I.G.P. Pavri and other senior police officials. They all take their place in the living room. Over the next thirty-five minutes, I provide them a detailed account of the last two days. They all listen to me intently. Babubhai is in tears. Hitubhai looks remorseful. The Governor sighs deeply.

Hitubhai looks at Madhavsinhbhai and says, 'We are calling in the armed forces now. The decision has been taken.'

Hours go by. Finally they all leave.

It is close to curfew time. The visitors have stopped coming. Today the curfew seems to have been imposed strictly. The road is completely deserted. The only visitors are ones with passes. Outside the house, under the neem tree, Madhavsinhbhai and I stretch out on the charpai.

It is evening. Some activist friends turn up. We get to hear all kinds of rumours. We also receive the news that a three-member commission appointed by the Indian Parliament will visit Ahmedabad.

The evening is giving away to night. Ishwarbhai's wife Jayaben accompanies Pratima to the living room where we all sit. They are our neighbours at the Ashram. Jayaben says, 'I am taking Pratima to my house. She is not well. She needs rest. Henceforth she should stay with me; that is what we have decided. I thought I should let you know. You don't worry about her.'

Pratima tells me, 'Gira has left Minita Apartment and come to be with Ba. She is looking after the children really well. They are also fond of her. So I am feeling quite relieved after handing over everything to her. You don't worry about anything. I am comfortable with this arrangement.'

Jayaben and Pratima leave after a while.

We continue to guard all night. We have revised the timing and made 2 am our limit for patrol.

The clock strikes 11 pm. With the desire to see the children, I go over to Shardaben's house. Anil Patel and another person accompany me. Shardaben is sitting and chatting with her neighbours, Ramiben and Chhaganbhai. They are speaking softly. On seeing us, Shardaben welcomes us, 'Come, come. The children are sleeping inside.' She opens the door softly. I go inside, leaving the door slightly ajar.

I find myself stepping into a familiar world. Long, whitewashed walls, a sloping Mangalore-tiled roof, stone flooring—the distinctive interiors of an Ashram house; simple, clean, and imbued with a quiet grace and dignity. I enter a familiar bedroom. The room is dark, except for the soft streaks of light from the night lamp. My eyes struggle in the dark for the vast *durri* on the floor with several mattresses spread out on it. On the left end is Gira, next to her is Bako, and hugging Bako is Kali. Laila is to the right, and the other children are in between.

I think of the contrast between the tense and turbulent world outside, and this soothing, safe haven inside. Seeing the children fast and safely asleep, I feel tranquil. I feel light as a flower. I shut the door quietly and leave.

I come back to Imam Manzil. We chat with friends and visitors. It is 2 am. Mansinghbhai, Mohanbhai, Madhavsinhbhai, Anil and I lie down on the large mat spread out upon the platform behind Imam Manzil.

We wake up at 5.30 am. By seven in the morning we are all bathed and ready. After many days we find the leisure to read the newspapers.

The curfew has been extended by another twenty-four hours.

The news about Akil Villa appears in the following manner in the *Times of India*:

> **Equality before law**
> After they broke open and ransacked a barrister's apartment in Navrangpura on Saturday night, hooligans set fire to the bookshelves. Besides volumes of law, in the blaze were burnt two books—the *Koran* and the *Ramayana*.

On the first page of *Times of India*, another shocking piece of news.

> **The last infamy**
> Not content with making them homeless, a violent mob at Vastrapur forced its hapless victims—mostly women—to leave behind all they had on their persons before fleeing. The inmates of a nearby university hostel came to their help with bedsheets.

Along with other news, there is also news of Shri Morarji Desai's expected arrival in Ahmedabad.

News on the radio mentions the lifting of the curfew between 10 am to 2 pm.

It is almost 10.30 pm. Surabhai arrives. He mentions that he and his companions had gone to drop a sadhu wanting to go to Hrishikesh to the Sabarmati railway station. They saw rioting mobs in the area of the powerhouse near the railway crossing. 'They stopped every car. The atmosphere was murderous. No one from the minority community is likely to escape in that area. Our car was also stopped and checked. We were shocked to see Home Guards in the rioting mob. We reprimanded them and asked them to make the crowd disperse, but no one was listening. We saw men openly carrying knives and spears. Two persons have been stabbed last night. Their dead bodies are lying outside the powerhouse. This area is likely to become explosive.'

There are signs of movement on the road since the curfew has been lifted.

Well-wishers continue to come and commiserate with us.

A long station wagon parks itself outside our home. A tall man in a white dhoti-kurta, koti and turban disembarks. Along with him is another individual in jodhpuris, and a third bearded person who looks like a maulvi, dressed in kurta-pyjama. 'Members of Parliament,' someone whispers. We all get up to receive them.

The three men, Shri Randhirsingh, Shri Chandrajit Yadav and Maulana Asad Miya Madni occupy the main seats in the living room. I apprise them of developments of the last few days. When I finish after half an hour, I see Chandrajit Yadav's eyes well up. The Parliament members express their sympathy. Maulana Madnisaheb seems to be in a hurry to leave.

Surabhai warns them of conditions in the Sabarmati station powerhouse area. Madnisaheb says, '*Chalo, us taraf chalein*, let us go in that direction.' The other members also intend to go in the same direction. We look at Madnisaheb's beard and try to dissuade him. But he is determined. They all leave.

Chandrajit Yadav bids farewell after a long and tight embrace. I am touched by his empathy.

The curfew is back. We see military trucks patrolling the streets now. Rifle-bearing army jawans have taken up positions. We come to know that Morarji Desai has undertaken a fast unto death to protest against the atmosphere of unrest.

Surabhai gets ready to leave. 'Some families have taken refuge in the open fields near Sola. They should be brought to Ahmedabad. Umarbhai from Sola called for help. He wants to meet in person.'

In the evening I come to know that a taxi coming from Kalol towards Sabarmati was set on fire. Most of the passengers died on the spot.

Night. Rumours contributing fear and tension continue to pour in. From Ranip, at a distance, screams continue to be heard.

It is almost midnight. We go to our respective beds. There is no end to the terrifying sounds. We see flashlights intermittently. Anil Patel and others are standing guard.

It is past twelve. A deathly silence prevails. It appears as if military trucks are patrolling the Ashram Road. We see three or four vans moving slowly in a row. From the van in front, someone is shouting into a loudspeaker: 'Strict curfew has been imposed. If you come out, you will be shot at sight.'

The words from the loudspeaker echo into the distance. A hush has fallen over the place.

I say to Madhavsinhbhai softly, 'Home Minister Chavan is coming tomorrow. That is why all this bandobast.'

Though time moves slowly, the days go by somehow. I have no idea of the day or date.

We slide into sleep.

We are awake, and it is morning.

Pratima comes over. 'Jayaben looks after me like her own daughter,' she says. Exhaustion, sleeplessness and anxiety over so many days have taken their toll—Pratima's health looks poor. At night she was much worse.

Madhavsinhbhai and I go to the Civil Hospital at midnight to get medicine for her. The roads are deserted. No sign of life anywhere, not a bird in sight or man. We have curfew passes with us. We show them at the Civil Hospital entrance. There we come to know that between ten in the morning and one in the afternoon when the curfew was relaxed, around thirty-seven dead bodies were brought to the hospital. 'Most of them had been in hiding for two days. But as the curfew was lifted they came out of their safe zones, and lost their lives.' We hear this from many people.

When will this massacre end?

We pick up the medicine from Civil Hospital and come home. Shamim rushes to us and says, 'You were not there, but Chavan Saheb had come to our place. It was like having the entire army over! A kafila of cars! Chavan Saheb came, Governor Saheb came, so did Hitubhai. Chandrajit Yadav came again. They all embraced Abba and left.'

This sympathy, affection and commiseration from the entire nation was touching indeed. It gave me a lot of courage.

The morning turns into noon. Surabhai comes and informs us that he helped people move to safer places from the riot-affected area of Sola.

Dhirubhai, his daughter and her little ones—Amit, Prashant and Anant—visit us. Dhirubhai mentions that he will be organising a prayer meeting at the Swastik Society Club the following day. He urges us to attend it.

The evening and night go by peacefully. The following day at around 11 am, we sit down for a meal. I am gripped by a sudden thought: today's newspaper mentions that Morarji Desai has lost weight as a consequence of his fast. I am wondering why I have lost weight despite eating regularly.

There is a charpai under the neem tree. After lunch, we lie down on the cot and rest. A green car pulls over. Waheedbhai, Mohanbhai and the driver Mathurji get down. Waheedbhai's two little daughters—four-year old Tinu and seven-year old Ruaab—leap out of the car. Mohanbhai has negotiated almost hundred and fifty kilometres one way and then back to bring Waheedbhai all the way from Taravada. Everyone is tired. Abba hugs Waheedbhai. Family members surround him and ask after his well-being.

There is a prayer meeting at Swastik Society in the evening. I am not sure if I want to take the children home. The house would be filled with burnt and broken objects, a site of violence and devastation. Witnessing such a sight would be traumatic for the children, wouldn't it? But the children insist on coming. They are longing to see their home. I am in a dilemma. I ask Madhavsinhbhai. He says, 'What is the harm if the children see all that? Creation has to emerge from all this destruction.

We need to rise and soar from the debris. It is important for the children to see this with their own eyes.' I see his point and decide to take the children along.

The clock strikes 4 pm. Madhavsinhbhai, Waheedbhai, Laila, Shirin, Ruaab, Pratima, Aabid, Kali, Munno, Naseem, Meena, Akil and myself—all of us go to Akil Villa.

Under the covered front yard of the bungalow lay a rope cot with a thin mattress spread over it occupied by Dhirubhai, who rushes to us and extends a warm welcome. I look at the warmth in his eyes. And I look at the torched and violated house next to him. My eyes dart towards the garden. Roses have blossomed. Dhirubhai goes and plucks some and brings them for me.

From the house opposite, Aabid's friend Ashok Nayak comes over. Six feet tall, the good-looking eighteen-year old lowers his eyes as he says to Pratima, 'Pratimaben, now you will never speak to us again, right? Why would you?' His voice is tear-filled; it has taken him some effort to speak.

Pratima says, 'Arre, how is that possible, bhai? Why must you say that?'

Ashok's eyes are downcast. 'I mean it. We could not save anything in your house. I realised that Aabid and I were from antithetical religions only when your house was burnt.'

Pratima tries to comfort a distressed Ashok. Ashok unlocks the house for us.

The last time I had seen the inside of the house was the night of the attack. Now I see it once again. 'In all these days, Ushaben has assiduously tried to clean up things and done the best she could,' Madhavsinhbhai tells me.

The newly-made book shelves in my office are burnt. The window frames are burnt. The roof is still hot. Outside, Aabid and Munna's burnt bicycles and tables and chair lie in a heap of ashes. All the burnt books lie in another heap in a corner.

The dining room objects are scattered all over.

The toy cupboard in the drawing room is in disarray. The beauty from Kashmir has been abducted; there is no trace of her existence anywhere. Caesar's head has fallen off; it lies in a corner, broken in two. The band party is in ruins; the drum has been flung at the far end of the room; no sign of the drummer, but one of his hands is still stuck on the drum. The army soldiers lie wounded, burnt and dead. The football players have melted. The row of policemen that decorated the shelf is in a sorry state. Were they inspired by the toy police officers that we saw in the city, quietly witnessing the violation of life and property? It must be that—the same example of dereliction of duty. Forget standing erect, they cannot even hold their heads high anymore.

Away from this heap of dismal destruction and beyond the half-shut door, there is one who still lies intact. He has neither been scorched by the blazing heat of the fire nor borne injury of any kind. Unnoticed, he has somehow escaped through the cracks when everything in sight was being burnt and broken. That droll fellow with a fancy cap on his head who can sway his body this way and that—the joker! We had perched him high on top of the almirah so he could always be visible and entertain us, but he had jumped off and escaped. I am gripped by a strong desire to preserve this dumb toy. I no longer feel any attachment towards all the toys and mementos I have collected between Kashmir and Madras on the one hand and between Dwarka and Assam on the other. But I suddenly feel a strong attachment, a *moha* towards this little comedian. I pick him up gently. I want him for safekeeping.

Pratima is riffling through the heap of burnt, torn, half-destroyed books. Her fingers make a quick dash and pick out a tiny red book from under the pile—*Rubaiyyat* of Omar Khayyam, gifted to me by Madhavsinhbhai. She puts it in my hand. It is damp, and has escaped the fire.

Prayer time is drawing near. All of us come out. Suddenly Akil comes running from the bedroom. He is holding a violin in his hands, his face beaming with joy. Before I can ask him, he says excitedly, 'Papa, Papa! My violin, Aabid's binoculars and Munna's microscope have survived!'

Not pain and grief, but joy and happiness! Not mourning over loss, but grateful joy at what has survived!

The beginnings of a sweet new life.

WRITING/TRANSLATING IN A DIVIDED WORLD

Go ask the setting sun
If he knows whose eyes would he drown in today?
And if he rises again like a bloodied dagger tomorrow
Whose chest would he stab?
Whose address would the death mail carry?
And who, pray, will hand deliver to whom?
Into hands that sweat and toil on fields
Who will place bloodthirsty weapons?
Who will now survive in this city that floats in fire and tears?
(Dhruv 2003: 75)

At the time of translating the above verse from the poetry of Saroop Dhruv, it was possible to say that the city that floats in fear and tears was Ahmedabad. Looking back, it seems somehow that many cities could join the list and the description would still stand valid. However the roots of communal hatred are particularly deep in Gujarat, our association with them has been much longer, and an entirely euphemistic language of common sense justifying the separation of communities well in place. Very little literature responds with poignancy to this division, and it has been my attempt to translate, or at any rate, foreground it. Translating *Agnipariksha* stems from the same motivation.

Translators, generally and especially in divided societies, are not mere specialists in linguistic and cognitive transfer, they are equally responsible and complicit in forms of exclusion and inclusion. In fact both writing and translation in divided times require a stepping out of one's textuality and ideology to communicate and listen. Dhruv's voice rung out, clear as a bell, while another writer Minal Dave (2003) created a fictional world and said a lot in a story. Titled 'Othaar' in Gujarati, and 'Nightmare' in English (Kothari 2007a) Dave's story focuses upon a well-meaning, almost liberal Hindu upper-caste woman travelling from what appears like Baroda to Ahmedabad. The curfew has just been lifted after communal riots in the city. The nervous and fearful protagonist's fears are intensified when she sees that her sole fellow traveler is a burkha-clad woman. However in the silence that follows, the two women recognise each other's fears, their vulnerabilities and the common context that binds them across borders of language and religion. The 'other' ceases to be the other and appears comforting as a mirror image. The two women step into each other's experiential textuality by moving out of their bodies—as translations are supposed to do—and create a sisterhood which holds in abeyance the claims of nations and ethnicities.

In a more recent time, the writer Ila Arab Mehta tells the story, not of riots, but of a peace resting upon a segregated world. Fateema Lokhandwala, the chief protagonist of the novel (Kothari 2015) grows as a restless young girl in rural Gujarat. Hungrily devouring books that come along and education that comes to her piecemeal in form of the scraps her father collects, she longs to jump the fence of poverty by educating herself and especially by learning the English language. While she becomes a professional in the city, a dream of living in a mixed locality with people from other religions grips her and the novel documents her tragic attempts at seeking this unattainable goal in an ostensibly modern and secular world. As a Hindu writer, Ila Mehta translates Fateema's experiences into writing, which was further translated into English in 2015. Fateema's resistance to being ghettoised is also a resistance to being defined and textualised in specific ways, and therefore translation assumes yet again many levels between the telling and re-telling of this story. Examples of such narratives are being provided to underscore how central both writing and translating are in reminding us of the exclusionary nature of 'normalcy' and how such acts must be seen as interventions, and not as mere projects and publications. *Agnipariksha* is for me a similar milestone in that journey, for it stems from the same set of motivations. It is also a valuable addition to the thin body within Gujarati literature that deals with the fissures characterising its social fabric. What is astounding about *Agnipariksha* is that it manages to do so without anger and bitterness, and when hints of such emotions do appear, they are directed at the state machinery and not at human beings. This characteristic of the book reflects the author's philosophy towards literature, which is that literature must deal with truth, but truth that elevates humanity without demonisation of the other. It is, as evident from Narayan Desai's preface, a mark of 'Gandhian' literature.

I

Documented like a live account over five to seven days in the month of September 1969, *Agnipariksha* details the experiences in first person of a well-heeled, respected Gujarat High Court lawyer who lived in both word and spirit a life of religious and cultural pluralism. Unprepared for the assaults on his life and property during the communal riots of 1969, Hamid Kureshi (hereafter, Hamidbhai) is taken aback by the extent of hatred directed at individuals like him. For the first time in his life he, a non-practising Muslim married to a Hindu woman, is reduced to being only a Muslim. The realisation dawned upon him that despite the social world of Gandhians that he belonged to, the influential individuals from the state and judiciary that he personally knew, the Hindu families he was not only friends with but also related to through marriage, and more importantly, despite his deep commitment to a life of *sarvadharmasamabhavna* or equal respect for all religions, he was not free of his identity.

Hamidbhai grew up in the city of Ahmedabad in a building called Imam Manzil that carries with it an illustrious history from the days of the Gandhi Ashram. An English and Hindi plaque outside the Imam Manzil mentions the following:

> The house in which Imam Abdul Kadir Bawazeer, who accompanied Gandhiji from South Africa in 1915 [and] stayed with him as his close associate and faithful co-worker until his death in 1931.

This is how Gandhi begins a biographical essay on Imam Saheb after the latter passed away:

> Imam Saheb went to South Africa about the same year as I (1893). His real name was Abdul Kadir Bawazeer, but, as he served as Imam in South Africa, most people knew him as Imam Saheb. I always addressed him by this name.
>
> The Imam Saheb's father was the Muezzin of the famous Jumma Masjid in Bombay and served in that capacity right till his death. He died only a few years ago, after the Imam Saheb's return to India. He fell dead just as he was washing and getting ready for the azan. Such a death comes only to the blessed. The Imam Saheb's forefathers were Arabs and had come to India and settled in the Konkan years ago. Hence he knew the Konkani language too. His mother tongue was Gujarati, but he had little schooling. He knew Arabic well enough to be able to read from the Koran Sharif with a pleasing intonation, though not so well as to be able to understand everything in the Koran. He had picked up, through contacts in practical life, English, Dutch and Creole French. Urdu, of course, he knew. He had also a working knowledge of Zulu. His intellect was so sharp that, if he had regularly studied in a school, he would have earned reputation as a great scholar. Though he was not a lawyer, he

> had come to understand subtleties of law through practical experience. (Gandhi 1932)

Given his commitment to the freedom struggle, Imam Saheb wanted his daughters to marry men who would be committed to the service of the nation and accept life at the Gandhi Ashram. When Hamidbhai's mother Ameena married Ghulam Rasool Kureshi (himself a Gandhian and down-to-earth man willing to lead life as an Ashramite), the invitation of the wedding dated 15 May 1924 was sent on behalf of Gandhi, written in his own words. Hamidbhai was one of the children of Ghulam Rasool Kureshi and Ameenaben. Hamidbhai grew up in Gandhi's proximity among the Ashramites and in a family whose devotion to the nation, and especially to Gandhi, was total. Newspapers in Ahmedabad (upon the death of Hamidbhai in October 2016) recounted instances of Hamidbhai's boyhood at the Ashram (see *The Indian Express*, 9 October 2016; and *The Times of India*, 9 October 2016).

In 1969, when Hamidbhai stood vulnerable and helpless, not only in his house at Swastik Society—hitherto unmarked by violence—but also in Imam Manzil, an entire legacy of Gandhian syncreticism and philosophy stood challenged by hatred and violence. The paradox of this book lies in this fact: both in the betrayal and in the restoration of faith. Finally when Hamidbhai and his family, including his father, sister and children, remain protected, it is thanks to the Ashram community. However, the fact that the Ashram community had no one else to turn to and that it could also become a target of communal hatred is the saddest moment of the narrative. The words, 'Gandhiji's Ashram has been attacked. No place is safe now' (p. 18) encapsulate the moment of shedding away of all hope in the civil society. Equally ironic and tragic is the fact that 1969 was the centenary of Gandhi's birth. The occasion was inaugurated in the state of Gujarat by Khan Abdul Ghaffar Khan, or Frontier Gandhi, who was distressed to see such destruction.

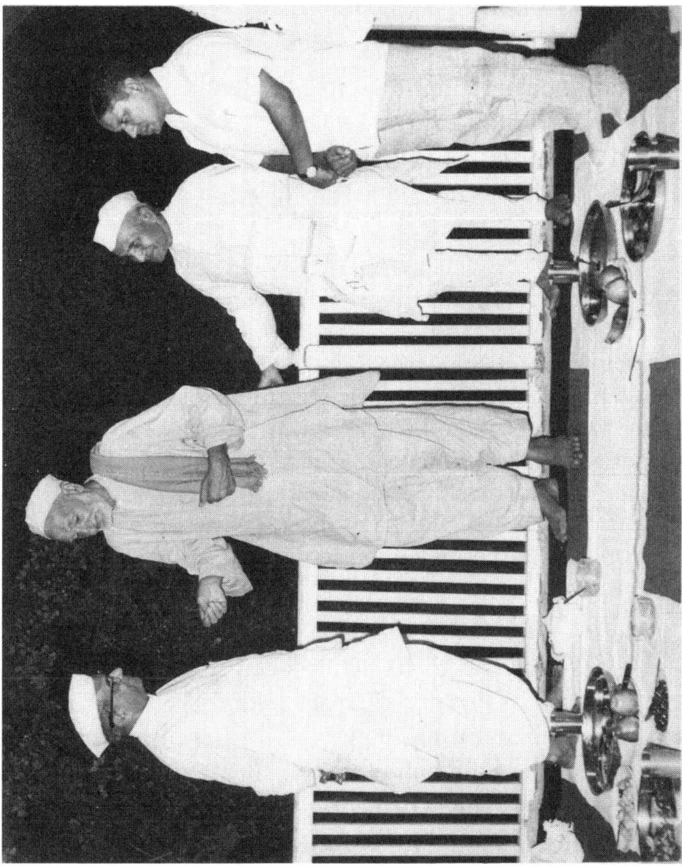

Hamid Kureshi meeting Khan Abdul Ghaffar Khan. *Courtesy*: Gira Kotak

II

Although the riots of 1969 extended beyond Ahmedabad, *Agniparikshа* is based entirely on events in that city. Hamidbhai's scene-by-scene narration of places he inhabits, visits, passes through, stops by and bypasses provides the cartography of a violence-ridden city. It is evident quite early in his account that Hamidbhai is taken by surprise at the revelation of this aspect of Ahmedabad. 'Not just communal strife, but violence? In my own city, in my own locality, my car is stopped and I am wounded? I am aghast.' This is not to say that riots were new to Ahmedabad. What is new is that their ambit and impunity have expanded. As Hamidbhai recounts:

> Scenes from 1941 and 1946 in Ahmedabad flash before my eyes. The coming together of the *Rathyatra* and Friday—scuffles, stabbing, bloodshed, the massacre of innocents. Images marked indelibly on a child's mind toss and turn. After finishing grade three in Gujarat Vidyapeeth I was admitted to C. N. Vidyavihar. Around that time, riots had broken out. Bloodthirsty demons had played havoc with the city of Ahmedabad. The atmosphere was vicious enough to turn even the best into monsters. (p. 8)

This time, the 'monsters' have intruded into the 'safe' zones of areas like Navrangpura where he lived, or the University area where his brother Waheedbhai lived.

Persisting as hair-raising memories in the minds of many Hindus and Muslims, the riots of 1969 are relatively under-served by researchers, especially when compared to the events of 2002. Through *Agniparikshа*, I came to the subject of the 1969 riots for the second time. The first time was when my attention was drawn to the participation of the Sindhi community in the riots (see Kothari 2007). Families such as that of Ehsan Jafri (killed during the 2002 riots) carry with them the memories of 1969. In a personal correspondence with me, Nishrin Jafri (Ehsan

Jafri's daughter) mentioned that while her father was silent on the subject, her mother Zakia Jafri would talk a lot about 1969. Zakia Jafri in 1969 was a young married woman who had come from Madhya Pradesh to live in Gujarat. It was shocking for her to witness the scale of violence. The process of ghettoisation of the Muslim community in Ahmedabad, and especially the emergence of Juhapura where Muslims increasingly began to seek refuge, began after the events of 1969. A longstanding friend Sadiq Noor Pathan mentions how 2002 was merely reminiscent of 1969, for by then we had seen the worst and learnt to keep silent. 'My son tells me you have made us timid,' but he doesn't know what happened to our psychology in 1969 (personal conversation, 20 September 2017).

If Ahmedabad seems unstudied from this point of view, other regions have almost entirely escaped documentation. It was once again conversations around the translation that brought to me the narratives of Amar Jesani and Vibhuti Patel, communicated to me by the latter. Amar Jesani is from the region of Amreli in Saurashtra. Now a well known bio-ethics expert and activist, Jesani was in his teens in 1969. His family went from being reasonably well off to lower middle class, and some of the vengeance came from people to whom his family had lent money as moneylenders. After losing home and property, Jesani's family moved to a Muslim mohalla. Meanwhile, Vibhuti Patel, a well known feminist and academic, mentions how as a fourteen-year old Hindu girl in the city of Baroda, she went through pitiless reflection on the violence and identified religion as one of its roots. From being a devout young Vaishnav girl she became an atheist, and life brought her and Amar Jesani in an overlapping circle of left-oriented activism in their later years. Despite belonging to different places and religions, 1969 was a life-changing event for both (personal conversation, 27 September 2017).

Yagnik and Sheth (2011) delineate a layered and complex background of the changing sociology and economics in the city of Ahmedabad in the decade of the 1960s. The Reddy Report—

put together after an inquiry committee was instituted under the chairmanship of Justice P. Jagmohan Reddy—remains to this day the most exhaustive account of this period. It mentions that the population of the city shows a rise from 12,06,001 to 18 lakhs from 1961 to 1969. The middle and upper class sections resided in the walled city of Ahmedabad as well as in Ellisbridge, Navrangpura, Sabarmati, Shahibag, Kankaria and Maninagar etc. While the labour and working class sections of the population resided in slums and in small blocks of brick-in-cement built by the Gujarat Housing Board in Amraiwadi, Dhudheshwar, Jahangirpur, Chamanpura, Saraspur, Rakhial, Gomtipur and Bapunagar etc. (Reddy Report 1969: 22). The influx of migrant labour from Rajasthan and Uttar Pradesh, the Indo-Pakistan war of 1965, the continued presence of extremist groups whose speeches incited communal feelings at rallies and a host of other factors in the immediate and remote past were taken into consideration by the inquiry committee. The committee also noted that not an inconsiderable role could have been played by organisations such as Hindu Dharma Raksha Samiti and Hullad Pidit Sahayata Samiti. One of the pieces of evidence produced before the Commission was the tape record of the speech made by Balraj Madhok, MP at Ahmedabad, on 14 September 1969 under the auspices of the Rifle Association on the subject of 'Pakistani Threat.' Madhok, who was examined as a witness by the Commission, acknowledged its authenticity (Reddy Report 1969: 33). Among the more immediate causes for the riots, the Report, the history by Yagnik and Sheth, and even *Agnipariksha* relate an incident of attack on the *mahants* of Jagannath temple on the morning of 18 September. At the same time the Report also mentions that:

> there is unanimity of opinion not only entertained by high police officers but also by public men that on the day of the Jagannath temple incident on the 18th of September 1969, the communal atmosphere in Ahmedabad city was not such that any of them expected riots to break out generally

> or spread in such manner and intensity as ultimately they turned out to be. (Reddy Report 1969: 43)

On the whole, the Reddy Report remains inconclusive in determining the exact role played by incidents of an immediate nature in the possible deterioration of the social fabric taking place over many years. Importantly, however, the places mentioned by Hamidbhai, such as the Shab-e-Burhani mosque and the *kabadi* bazar among others, also find a mention in the Report.

To my mind, a significant aspect of *Agnipariksha*—supported by the Reddy Report—is the delay in restoring law and order in the city. We notice in the narrative that despite several calls made by Hamidbhai and his friend and former minister, Madhavsinh Solanki, police protection is not promptly provided. In fact in a painful enumeration of violent incidents, Hamidbhai's tone acquires an anger and sarcasm when he observes the passivity of the police:

> "Where there is police, there is peace." I think of the irony of these words and feel it is more in the spirit of: "Where there is peace, there is police." Surely they would not be able to say that there was peace where they were. I wondered if the inanimate cops I saw earlier were better than these fugitives ones. (p. 11)

Why were there delays, and how do we understand this failure of the state? These questions remain unanswered in *Agnipariksha*.

III

Agnipariksha is dedicated to Narayanbhai, who lived in the slums of Gulbai Tekra in Ahmedabad. It is also dedicated to Kamu, who was employed by Hamid Kureshi's family to do the housework, Kamu's husband Kaluji, and to all those who stood by Hamid Kureshi in testing times, including his late wife Pratima.

Hamid Kureshi with his wife Pratima at their charred home in 1969.
Courtesy: Gira Kotak

Furthermore, Hamid Kureshi would have liked to mention Vinod Bhatt who inspired him to publish *Agnipariksha* and have its English translation see the light of day.

As a translator of this text, I would like to thank Sangam House for providing me with a tranquil environment to work in. I thank Gira Kotak, Hamidbhai's sister-in-law and close friend whose involvement in this text has been next to none. The fact that this book is part of a Gandhi Studies series brought under the aegis of Orient BlackSwan is a matter of pride. It is a fitting appreciation of Hamidbhai's approach to life, and of his friends at the Ashram and otherwise who stood by him. This valuable glimpse of civil society in the 1960s has been rarer in the subsequent years.

Meanwhile, let down by many and helped by many, Hamid Kureshi prefers to name only those who stood by him, even in the book. The former to his mind constitute a mass of anger and he chooses not to think of them in specific terms. As for a state that does not seem to be moved by his frequent pleas for help, at least for the first four days of the riots, Hamidbhai hints at its passivity but maintains a studied silence on individual motivations. The parallels this narrative has with our own times are uncanny and deeply disturbing. Hamidbhai's dignity deterred him from mudslinging, and for better or worse, the translation must also be read in the spirit of that decision and dignity. Jim Zanetto, a friend living in the United States, asks Hamidbhai in a letter:

> The primary question I have for you is, What now for Ahmedabad and the surrounding region? You have created a literary work around a social/political series of events. You have steadfastly refrained from making any political judgments or recommendations. The power of your work is based on the humanistic perspective of personal and family survival within a life-threatening chaos. Is it too dangerous, or too unfathomable to add a chapter, or perhaps write a separate essay on the social and political aspects of the current situation? Looking back 35 years later, and summarizing the events between then and now,

> what is your sense of the situation? Are there situations that Gandhi faced that are relevant? (Zanetto 2004)

Agnipariksha was brought out in print in 2003. It is evident from the letters (addressed to Hamidbhai) written by leading literary figures in Gujarat that *Agnipariksha* had touched the hearts of all those who read it. Whether the same individuals have had the courage to speak up against the state or not is a separate matter. In unequivocal terms, many writers of Gujarat identified *Agnipariksha* as a fine example of Gandhian literature, and an essential text for bridging the gap between Hindus and Muslims.

Did the unfortunate massacres of 2002 inspire Hamidbhai to bring this account into the public domain? The writer, Keshubhai Desai points out, 'Hamid Kureshi buried his suffering for twenty-three years. The able lawyer who suppressed his personal grief for so many years begs examination. The post-Godhra events perhaps compelled him to dig out the file he must have put away in a loft and remove the dust gathered over it for three decades' (Desai, p. 1–2). Was the inseparability of 1969 from 2002 one of the animating contexts? Or was it the possibility that *Agnipariksha* could become in the beastly atmosphere of 2002 a document testifying human kindness? Upon receiving the manuscript of *Agnipariksha*, the writer Ratilal Borisagar mentions how his first response was to say to Hamid Kureshi: Why open old wounds? However upon reading the book, Borisagar realised that when all else failed for Hamidbhai, including the state institutions, it was the Ashram community, Hindu friends and Hindu neighbours who put their lives at risk and stood by him and his family. And that is why, 'this is an important lesson of communal harmony.'

An intense desire to have this story disseminated gripped Hamidbhai in the later years of his life. On 26 September 2016, he went through the first draft of this translation with me. The tentatively put English title 'Trial by Fire' made him uncomfortable. 'It was a test at many levels, it wasn't just about the fact that my house was burnt down,' he said. I did not argue that the English title was only a literal translation of the Gujarati

Agnipariksha, which also includes the word, 'fire.' If *agni* is both physical and metaphoric, why would that not be so in English as well, I wondered. Why did Hamidbhai find 'fire' so crude? Thinking of discussing this with him another time, I left. Twelve days later, on 8 October 2016, I heard that Hamidbhai was no more. The book retains its original title; the credit for the English subtitle goes to Ramchandra Guha.

Rita Kothari

References

Borisagar, Ratilal. 2003. Personal correspondence with Hamid Kureshi. Letter dated April.

Desai, Keshubhai. Undated. 'Gandhivichaarni Agnipariksha.' Khevna.

Dhruv, Saroop. 2003. *Hastakshep* [Intervention]. Translated from the Gujarati by Rita Kothari. Ahmedabad: Samvedan Sanskritik Manch.

Gandhi, M. K. 1932. '101. Imam Saheb-I,' 7 March 1932. In *The Collected Works of Mahatma Gandhi*. Vol. 55: 10 February 1932–15 June 1932, p. 106. New Delhi: Publications Division, Government of India, 1999 (Electronic Book).

Kothari, Rita. 2007a. 'Nightmare.' In *Katha: Short Stories by Indian Women*, ed. Urvashi Butalia. Delhi: Stanza.

———. 2007b. *The Burden of Refuge: Sindhi Hindus of Gujarat*. Delhi: Orient BlackSwan.

———. 2015. *Fence*. Ila Arab Mehta. Translated from the Gujarati. Delhi: Zubaan Books.

Reddy Report. 1969. Inquiry into the Communal Disturbances at Ahmedabad and Other Places in Gujarat on and after 18th September, 1969. Instituted under Home Department, Notification No.GG/1722/SB. III/COI.1069. Dated 13 October 1969.

Yagnik, Achyut, and Suchitra Sheth. 2011. *Ahmedabad: From Royal City to Mega City*. Delhi: Penguin Books.

Zanetto, Jim. 2004. Personal correspondence with Hamid Kureshi. Letter dated 12 October.